Call Center Optimization

Call Center Optimization

Ger Koole

MG books
Amsterdam

Preface

This book is written for everybody who is dedicated to improving call center performance. It offers a rational, scientific method to the understanding and optimization of call centers. It explains all generic aspects of call and contact centers, from the basic Erlang formula to advanced topics such as skill-based routing and multi-channel environments. It does this without going into technical details, but by showing the outcomes of many calculations. Moreover, there is a companion web site where these calculations can be executed for different input values. Next to understanding call center phenomena we show how to use these insights to improve call center performance in a systematic way. Keywords are data collection, scenario analysis, and simulation.

This book is a bridge between call center management and those parts of mathematics that are useful for call centers. It shows the manager and consultant the benefits of an analytical approach, without having to go into the technical details of it. It also shows the mathematically educated reader an interesting application area of queueing theory and other fields of mathematics. As such, this book can well be used as additional material in an applied course for mathematics and industrial engineering students. Basic knowledge of call centers is assumed, although a glossary is added in case of omissions.

There are many people who helped me writing this book. I would like to thank in particular Karin van Eeden, Theo Peek, Roger Rutherford, and Arnout Wattel for their suggestions, and Marco Bijvank, Joeri van Hoeve, Auke Pot and Alex Roubos for their help with the online tools. I would also like to thank all organizations that allowed me to use their data.

I started this project in 2001. It was hard to find time next to my regular obligations, so I found myself writing during holidays and scientific visits at various locations. At the same time, my understanding of call centers progressed and I changed several times the way the text is set up. Christmas 2012 was the ideal moment to finish. Altogether, it was an extremely interesting experience to write this book. I hope that you will find it equally rewarding to read it.

Ger Koole
Amsterdam/Amstelveen/Sophia Antipolis/le Croisic/Courdemanges
2001–2013

Contents

Chapter 1

Introduction

This chapter introduces the ideas and concepts that we will use throughout this book. It does so by concentrating on one specific part of call center optimization, workforce management (WFM), and more specifically on the determination of the number of agents that need to be scheduled to satisfy a certain service level. Next to introducing the ideas and concepts, it serves as an introduction to the following chapters in which the different parts of WFM are discussed in full detail. In Chapter 9 call center optimization outside of WFM is discussed.

There is no need to worry if this chapter raises more questions than it anwers. All questions will (hopefully) be answered in the subsequent chapters.

1.1   Workforce management

The activity where analytical techniques are used most often is WFM. WFM is the common name of the planning cycle that results in the schedules of the call center agents, usually a few weeks before the period (often a week) for which the schedule is made. As input it uses historic call center data on traffic loads and information on agent availability; the output consists of agent schedules.

WFM can be split into several more or less separate steps. The first is forecasting the traffic load. This needs to be done at the level of time intervals of usually 15 or 30 minutes. A forecast is easily made, but producing accurate forecasts is a complicated task that requires considerable skills and knowledge. Good forecasting is crucial for good WFM, following the GIGO principle: if you start the WFM with bad input ("garbage in"), then irrevocably the resulting schedule will be of bad quality ("garbage out"). What makes good forecasting difficult are the many factors that influence arriving call volume, and the fact that due to the random nature of the call arrival process one can never be completely sure what the causes were of observed fluctuations.

The second step in WFM is determining the required staffing levels for each interval. Sometimes this is considered to be part of forecasting, but it is at this point in the WFM process that demand and supply are matched: here it is determined how many agents (and possibly which types of agents) are needed at every interval to obtain the required service level. In simple single-skill call centers with only inbound calls the so-called *Erlang C formula* is often used for this. For more complicated operations with multiple skills and other communication channels such as email more advanced techniques such as *simulation* have to be used to evaluate staffing levels accurately. Often however rough approximations are used that give unreliable results. In the next sections we will introduce in more detail simulation and the Erlang formula.

Next we have to turn the staffing levels into agent schedules or rosters. This is the scheduling step. It can be done in two different ways. In the first agents specify their preferences beforehand and an advanced algorithm does the assignment taking all constraints (as much as possible) into account. The second consists of agents choosing the shift that they prefer on the basis of some auction system. The latter method is called *shift bidding*, and works best when the number of different types of shifts is limited.

Integrating staffing and scheduling

It often occurs, due to the relative inflexibilty of shifts, that the requirement to satisfy the service levels in each interval leads to considerable overstaffing at certain moments. This happens for example if there is a short spike in call volume or if all shifts overlap at some moment. The overall service level is then considerably higher than necessary. This can be avoided by integrating the staffing and scheduling steps.

Unfortunately WFM does not end with making shifts. Things not always go as planned, and adaptations have to be made. Both changes in call volume and scheduled agents can occur. An important operational task is monitoring *schedule adherence* and reacting accordingly. When call volume is different than expected, then also changes have to be made. This activity is often called *traffic managament*, although in many cases it is the traffic that is monitored but the workforce that is managed. The whole is called *real-time performance management*.

Management, planning and scheduling

Management is a very broad term including all aspects of accomplishing organizational goals. WFM, as just described, is a much more narrow activity. To cite an expert: "Workforce management is the codeword for forecasting and scheduling software in the contact center industry" [12]. In fact, workforce *scheduling* would be a much better term instead of WFM: scheduling is about assigning tasks to resources, in this case agents. When considering also the other subjects treated in this book then the term *planning* fits best. For example, setting up a rational data-based long-term policy concerning the hiring and training of new agents is clearly planning, but not scheduling.

Agent scheduling is a crucial activity in any call center, without agent schedules the call center cannot operate. Without adequate software it is a laborious activity, especially in bigger call centers. This is the main reason why agent scheduling is automized in many centers, and why many software tools exist for this task. The core consists of algorithms supporting the different steps of WFM, but to make it work efficiently many more modules are necessary: a database filled with historical call volumes, data with agent information, connections with many other systems such as the ACD to get traffic information, and so forth. Next to that, a number of the larger WFM tools are part of software suites that offer other functionality such as email handling.

The functionality of these WFM tools varies enormously, and so does the quality of the proposed solutions. In practice we see that many tools are only partly used, and that users have their own, often Excel-based solutions, for, for example, forecasting and staffing. When selecting a new WFM tool organizations usually mostly look only at the functionality, little or not at the way certain methods are implemented. Every WFM tools has the possibility to forecast call volume, but the quality of the forecasts depends on the tool. Another example is that most WFM tools support multi-skill call centers, but the way in which it is implemented in the scheduling module varies also from tool to tool, and with that the quality of the resulting schedules. One of the objectives of this book is to develop a more critical look at WFM and thereby help the reader make better use of WFM tools.

1.2 The Erlang C formula

In this section and the following ones we consider the staffing of a single-skill inbound call center. We are interested in computing the optimal staffing level, let's say defined as the minimal number of agents required to answer 80% of the calls within 20 seconds. To do so we have to be able to predict the service level (SL) for a fixed number of agents, and then by varying the number of agents we can find the right staffing level. Our prediction of the service level will evidently depend on a number of variables: the forecast (FC) of the call volume, the number of agents, and also the average call handling time (AHT). Probably we are interested in staffing levels for a whole day or longer, but because forecasts and therefore also staffing levels vary over the day we concentrate on an interval of 15 or 30 minutes.

The FC is usually given per interval. To have everything in the same unit we divide by the length of the interval to get the FC per minute. Let us use the greek letter λ for this number (following a perhaps seemingly strange mathematical habit). Similarly, we denote by β the AHT, also in minutes. Then $\lambda \times \beta$ is called the offered load. This is equal to the number of agents needed to be able to handle all incoming calls. However, calls arrive at random moments, and therefore somewhat clustered, and handling times vary. Thus, if you have no or hardly any overstaffing with respect to the offered load, then the service level will suffer from these short random periods of high load. It is the Erlang C formula that gives the relation between FC, AHT, number of agents and service level, taking the randomness into account. The bad news is that this is not a simple relation that anybody can learn. The good news is that the Erlang formula has already been implemented in different spreadsheet add-ins, WFM solutions and other tools.

Example   *Consider a call center with a FC of 100 for the 10:00-10:15 interval. The AHT is 3:30. Then $\lambda = 100/15 = 6.66$ and $\beta = 3.5$. The load is thus $6.66 \times 3.5 = 23.33$, and the minimum number of agents required to handle all calls is 24. The Erlang C formula predicts that in that situation only around 21% of all calls wait less than 20 seconds before getting connected. By increasing one by one the number of agents we find that 28 agents are needed to have a SL of at least 80%.*

In Chapter 4 we will study the Erlang C formula in more detail. However, there are also certain disadvantages to using the Erlang formula. The reason is that for the Erlang C calculation reality has been simplified. Certain statistical assumptions are made and certain features of call centers are left out. Without these assumptions and simplifications it is not possible to

---

Do it yourself

There are several Erlang C calculators that can be found on the web. There is also one that is especially designed to accompany this book at www.gerkoole.com/CCO. You can go there and try to reproduce the numbers of the example. We will make extensive use of this and other tools in this book.

---

compute the formula, but they can lead to considerable discreprencies between prediction and reality. For example, an important feauture that is not part of the Erlang C model is that some calls, while waiting for service in queue, abandon. In situations where little calls abandon this is not necessarily a problem, but especially in underload situations this might result in big prediction errors. Under certain statistical assumptions the model including abandonments, called the Erlang X model, can be solved (see Chapter 4).

Next we consider a different feature of the Erlang formula that can lead to considerable errors. To understand this, we should realize that the performance of call centers is not completely predictable. For example, consider the handling times. We know the average handling time (AHT) and probably some other statistical properties. However, we do not know the exact duration of the call that is to arrive next. That means that any two intervals, even if all parameters such as the FC and number of agents are equal, will have a different performance. This has important consequences for call center management: we always have to deal with unpredictable fluctuations. It also means that we have to take into account the unpredictability when making service level predictions. However, the Erlang C formula gives as output a single number, and no indication of the size of the error. This is because the Erlang C fomula gives the performance as if the call center would run with the same parameters for a very long time. In reality this is not the case, usually we consider 15 or 30 minute intervals at a time. For this reason we should expect variability in the SL. A method that allows to quantify the SL variability, and also many other features, is *simulation*.

1.3 Simulation

The central idea of computer simulation is that we mimic reality in the computer. That is, we generate, on the basis of the forecast, arrival moments. These calls are assigned to virtual agents, or queued if no agents are available. Agents finish serving when the handling times are over, and they start with a new call or become idle, depending on the situation. Possible other features include calls abandoning. Time progesses as events happen until the simulation time is over. All the while, statistics are assembled, for example on the number of calls that are answered within 20 seconds. Finally the required performance measures are calculated.

Because of the unpredictability, any two runs of the simulation are different, even when all input values are the same. In fact, if we take for example SL, any outcome is always possible. In a highly understaffed call center it might be that all calls need incidentally very little time leading to a high SL; conversely, in a well-dimensioned call center, it might occur that the first calls have very long handling times leading to congestion and a low SL. However, these situations are less likely to occur. Thus, when repeating the simulation often enough, we will see that the outcomes are concentrated around a certain level, apart from a number of outliers. This level is close to the level that is predicted by the Erlang model. In Figure 1.1 we plotted a histogram of 100 runs for the system of Example 1.2 with 28 agents. Note that the Erlang C formula predicts a SL of 83%, which falls within the 80-85% interval with the highest number of occurences, 34. (In Chapter 4 we will sharpen our understanding and see that the long run times, 8 hours, is crucial for this result.)

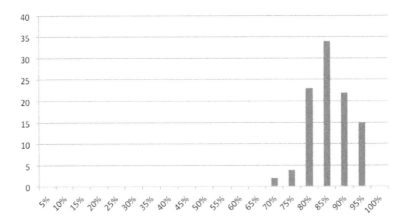

Figure 1.1: SL histogram for 100 runs of 8 hours

The calculations of Figure 1.1 were based on the Erlang C system. Using simulation it is easy to extend the model with features such as abandonments, different statistical assumptions underlying the handling times, different agents working at different speeds, redials, and so forth. When extending to systems with different skills with skill-based routing (SBR), simulation really becomes essential. No equivalent for the Erlang formula exists in this situation, and except for some unreliable estimations simulation is the only method that can be used, both for staffing decisions (in which we vary the number and skills of the agents) and determining the best call routing parameters. Please note that the last activity is not part of the WFM cycle but can clearly be approached by similar techniques. SBR is discussed in Chapter 6.

Simulation can be used instead of the Erlang formula to obtain staffing levels, which can be used to determine the agent schedules in the scheduling step. Certain tools use an integrated procedure where new solutions are evaluated using simulation, on the basis of which again new solutions are selected, etc. The question remains how to deal with the fact that every simulation run will give a different result. In fact, the question to be answered first is how to deal with the fact that performance in reality will vary from day to day, even if the parameters remain the same. Does this mean that performance prediction is useless, because the outcomes will be different anyway?

Of course, performance prediction is useful, because the outcomes are often close to the prediction (in a statistical sense, which will be precised). Thus, to avoid having to change too much during the day, it is reasonable to base the schedule on some form of average performance. This is the type of average which is calculated by the Erlang C formula and which can also be obtained by simulation, by averaging over many runs. Unfortunately, the precision of simulation outcomes increases slowly with the number of runs, revealing the main problem of simulation: to obtain a high precision for the prediction run times can become very long. This is a big difference with formulas such as the Erlang C, which produce answers within split seconds. Especially in situations where interactively the best solution is sought simulation can lead to very long execution times, to low quality solutions, or to both. Highly skilled mathematicians and software engineers are needed to design and build WFM systems that use this method. But, even if a highly reliable estimate is obtained, we should never forget that real-time performance management will always be necessary, to deal with random fluctuations and other more or less unpredictable events such as agent absence and forecasting errors.

> **Integrating scheduling and real-time performance management**
> In theory, the best thing to do would be to integrate the schedule and the real-time performance management steps as well. Then exactly the right amount of flexibility is scheduled, and over or understaffing with respect to the average staffing levels will be chosen optimally. At several research centers around the world scientist are developing these methods.

1.4   Call center optimization

Optimizing a call center is more than doing WFM the best possible way. There are many decisions that can benefit from a rational data-driven optimization approach. Some of these concern repetitive operational problems such as WFM, others are of a more ad hoc nature. The former are therefore executed by dedicated people that count these activities as (one of) their main tasks, the latter require specialists who can apply their analytical skills to many different problems.

A first class of problems are those the enable good WFM. A good long-term hiring policy, skill-based routing, and the right mix of employee contract types is essential for good WFM. In outsourcing contracts the payments depend on the actual traffic, but often also on the difference between the forecast and the actual traffic. Thus knowledge of forecasting, and of forecasting errors, is crucial to call centers who outsource (part of) their traffic. All these issues will be discussed in the relevant chapters related to WFM.

WFM is sometimes criticized that it focuses only on efficiency, not on quality. The promise of *workforce optimization* (WFO) is to remedy this problem. WFO refers to software suites that include, next to WFM, modules for quality monitoring and call recording, (agent) performance management, and eLearning. We discuss the analytics of these activities in Chapter 9.

There are many activities that can be thought of that are not yet part of call center software, but that would give a company a competitive advantage when addressing. Optimizing a call center means seizing also these opportunities. All activities together is what we call call center optimization.

1.5   Further reading

Reynolds [25] is an excellent introduction to WFM. Cleveland & Mayben [10] is less of an overview, but easier to read, and it contains many interesting insights.

For a list with the major WFM tools see Rosenberg [27].

The book [8] contains the historical background of Erlang's work.

Gans et al. [16] and Akşin et al. [2] are overviews giving the state of the art concerning mathematical models relevant to call center management. Both are written for academics, and assume solid mathematical knowledge. Stolletz [34] is also more mathematical.

Chapter 2

Performance measures and customer behavior

This chapter starts by defining the goals of customer contact and the way it is linked to customer behavior. Then we consider call center data. We discuss how to derive useful performance indicators from the data, considering both quality of service and efficiency. The outcomes of this chapter will serve as objectives and input parameters of the chapters on WFM and as a basis for the treatment of call center optimization in general in Chapter 9.

2.1   Call center objectives

Products are characterized by quality and price. The quality of a product might have many different aspects. In a production environment where tangible products are made, many aspects are related to what we might call the product itself. When we consider a TV set, this could be the size of the screen, the quality of the sound, and so forth. But there are also aspects that are not directly related to the product itself, such as the delivery conditions and the shopping experience (for example, whether it is bought online or in a shop). With customer contact a similar situation exists: certain aspects are related to the contact itself, certain are related to the way it is delivered. Examples of the former are the quality of the answer and the politeness of the call center agent, an example of the latter is the time that a customer has to wait before being connected to an agent.

   With customer contact it rarely occurs that callers pay directly for the call. An example of an exception is a directory service. Instead, call centers are mainly used to support certain business functions such as sales or product support. Then the customer pays indirectly for the call center when buying the product for which sales or service calls are done. In the case of outsourcing, calls directly generate the revenue, but it is not the caller who pays. Whatever the situation, high call center costs will translate, directly or indirectly, into a high price for the product concerned. Controlling costs is therefore essential. Whatever the revenue model is for the call center, the bigger part of its costs are personnel costs. They usually account for around 70% of the total costs.

To be able to improve the quality of a product and/or reduce its costs, we have to able to measure the quality and the costs. To do so we use *performance indicators* (PIs). These PIs are used in two ways: internally in the call center, that is, as input to our analytical techniques, and to communicate with stake holders outside of the call center. We have three types of PIs: those that are related to the costs of customer contact, those that are related to the quality of the contact, and those that are related to the way customer contact is delivered. For the latter often *service level agreements* (SLAs) are used.

Service level is an ambiguous term, especially in call centers. In its general sense it refers the quality of a product, especially to the non-product related properties such as waiting time. An example of a service level agreement is that the abandonment rate should not exceed 5%, 80% of the calls should be answered within 20 seconds, and the FCR rate should be at least 90%. To meet or exceed these objectives a certain budget is made available in case it concerns an internal call center. In case of an outsourcer the revenue depends on the extend to which the SLA is met. Usually a penalty is applied when the service level is lower than agreed upon.

The aspects of a product by which its quality is defined should also be chosen such that they can be measured. Some aspects are relatively easy to measure, such as the waiting time of a call. Some are harder to measure, such as the friendliness of the agent or the *First Call Resolution* (FCR) rate. Sometimes they require laborious data analysis or the use of advanced analytical tools, as can be the case for the FCR rate. In other situations customer surveys are needed, for example by automatically asking part of the customers for their opinion about the friendliness of the agent.

Costs can also be measured in PIs. One could think that total costs are the only relevant factor, but this not account for factors that influence the

---

Adverse effects of steering on PIs

It is good that performance is measured using PIs, but they should not become a goal by themselves. In that case they can even deteriorate quality of service. For example, if agents are stimulated for having short handling times, then they might be tempted to interrupt conversations before they are ended. In certain call centers it happens that agents are financially rewarded for, essentially, cutting calls after a few seconds. Analyzing call data reveals this type of practice. Another example of adverse effects of purely steering on PIs can be found in outsourcing. If an outsourcer is rewarded on the basis of SL, then there is no reason to answer calls who have waited longer than the service level limit. Thus it is "optimal" not to serve calls that have waited some time and wait until they abandon.

---

costs such as growth. Next, it does not give insight in the functioning of the call center. Given the fact that personnel costs represent the bigger part of the total costs we should use PIs that are related to the efficient use of the workforce.

When business problems are solved using software systems, as it is the case with WFM, it is very important to define the optimization goals clearly. In the next sections, we focus on the PIs that play an important role in WFM.

2.2   Customer behavior

To be able to choose an appriopate SL definition we have to understand customer behavior, as this reflects customer preferences. For example, if customers abandon very quickly, then we conclude that our callers are very impatient. This might lead us to choose a small "time-to-answer". In this section we consider that part of customer behavior that is relevant to WFM: handling times, patience, *redials* and *reconnects*. We make the following difference between redials and reconnects: when a customer calls again after having abandoned then it is a redial; when a customer calls again after having being served then it is a reconnect. To analyze these aspects of customer behavior in all details we need to have access to data at the individual call level. This is not always available in call centers: ACD reports are usually aggregated at the interval level, and it is not always possible to get call-level data.

Let us start by studying the handling times. The most important figure is the average, the AHT. However, it is also interesting to look at the *distribution* by making a histogram as in Figure 2.1. A statistical study of

---

The cost-quality trade-off

The manager of a call center tries to satisfy the service levels set by higher management, given the call center's budget, and other constraints such as the number of work places (often called seats), the ICT infrastructure, and the available workforce. Of course, the higher the budget, the higher the service level can be, due to better training and more available resources. The main resource is the call center agent or representative, although communication costs can also be high, certainly for toll-free services. This means that the (infra)structure and processes of a call center should be such that the effectiveness and efficiency of the workforce is maximized.

The cost-service level trade-off thus has a central place in quantitative call center management. In general, when costs increase, then the service level (SL) increases. Thus we can draw a graph in which we show the SL as a function of the costs. This is called the *efficiency curve*, see the figure below for the typicaL form. Note that the curve is flattening as the costs increase. We often see these *diminishing returns*. Where the efficiency curve lies depends on the SL definition, but also on the infrastructure and the processes: every call center has its own efficiency curve. Improving the call center infrastructure and processes will shift the efficiency curve up and/or to the left.

Efficiency curve

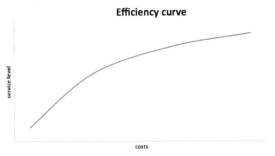

In certain situations the profit of each individual call can be measured in terms of money. In such a situation the average profit per handled call can be calculated, and instead of balancing cost and service level, we just maximize profit. We will pay attention to this business model in Chapter 4.

---

several call centers revealed that the handling time distribution is often well approximated by a so-called *log-normal* distribution. From a practical point of view, it is more relevant to note that the AHT varies in time (time of day, day of week) and with the agent. This has consequences for WFM: in a call center it should certainly be considered to use time-dependent AHTs, and also the longer AHTs of new agents should be accounted for. The differences between AHT are also interesting to study, mainly from a perspective of WFO. We will do this in Chapter 9.

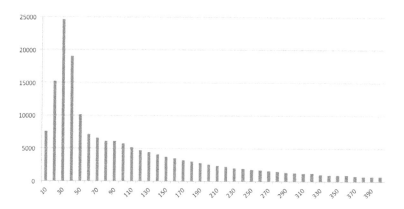

Figure 2.1: Histogram of handling time in a particular call center (in seconds)

Histograms and distributions

A histogram is made directly from a dataset: all outcomes are classified in "buckets" of equal length and the height of a bucket corresponds to the number of data points in the bucket. When the number of points is doubled, then the histogram becomes twice as high. When all numbers in the histogram are divided by the sum of the numbers then we get a distribution. The idea behind that is that these numbers can be used as approximations that the next data point will fall within the corresponding bucket. The validity of these type of questions are studied in statistics, as well as question whether the distribution ressembles some known form (such as the *normal distribution*). In general we can say that the more data points we have the better the approximation is, assuming that the circumstances have not been changed.

As an example, take the data set $\{0.5, 0.8, 1.2, 2.3, 2.5, 4.2, 5.1, 5.8, 6.1, 9.5\}$, and let's use buckets of length 1. Then the histogram and distribution are as in the figures below. The only difference is the verticale scale of the figure.

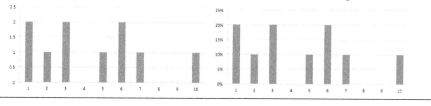

Next we consider abandonment behavior. Every caller will eventually abandon when not served, but the patience, the time that a customer is willing to wait in queue, differs between customers. Abandonments have both a

---

Percentages and probabilities

Percentages can used just as probabilities and as fractions, the difference being that a percentage is 100 times higher than the corresponding probability or fraction. For example, the statement "there is a 5% change that the actual is more than 10% higher than the forecast", is equivalent to the statement "the probability that the actual is more than 0.1 higher than the forecast is 0.05". Mathematicians prefer probabilities, because they can be multiplied: if the probability of a high actual is 0.3, and the probability of high absenteeism is 0.2, then the probability of both occuring is $0.3 \times 0.2 = 0.06$. Multiplication of probabilities is only allowed if the events are uncorrelated, that they are not likely to occur together because one is a consequence of the other, or because there is an underlying event that causes both. As an example of the latter, take two lines, each with a probability of 0.1 that the actual is high. Then the probability of high traffic on both lines is often higher that 0.01, because there are underlying causes such as weather conditions that may cause high traffic on both lines.

---

negative and a positive effect on the call center: negative because a call has not been handled, positive because it reduces congestion. In a call center most calls get served, thus we only know the patience of a small percentage of calls: the others get connected. However, the fact that they got connected gives information on their patience: it was longer than their waiting times. Not taking into account the effect of the connected calls can give a big error when estimating patience.

Example   *Consider a call center with a small group (5%) of calls with short patience (less than 30 seconds). The other callers have a patience that is more than 2 minutes. If the waiting time is usually around 1 minute, then we measure about 5% abandonments with an average patience less than 30 seconds. However, the patience measured over all calls is around 2 minutes or higher.*

On the basis of the patience of abandoned calls and the waiting time of connected calls we can make a statistical estimate of the patience distribution using the so-called *Kaplan-Meier estimate*. The idea behind this method is explained in the box below, but let us first look at some outcomes in Figure 2.2. There are three graphs in this figure, all based on the same data set. The first is the patience distribution based solely on the abandoned calls. The second is the statistically correct distribution, after applying the Kaplan-Meier method to the numbers. As we can see the histogram has shifted to the right, meaning that the patience is longer then we would expect based solely on abandoned calls. The third graph needs some clarification. Next to knowing that "7% of callers have a patience between 3:30 and 4:00", it might be of interest to know that "11% of callers who have waited for 3:30 are likely to abandon in the next 30 seconds". This so-called *conditional probability* (conditional on the fact that the caller has waited 3:30) is the third graph in the figure. It is surprising to see that after an initial high level the conditional probabilities stabilize. Apparantly there are two types of callers: those who abandon quickly and a larger group with a longer patience of which aboutt he same percentage abandon every time interval. This is of interest to our discussion of service level definitions later on.

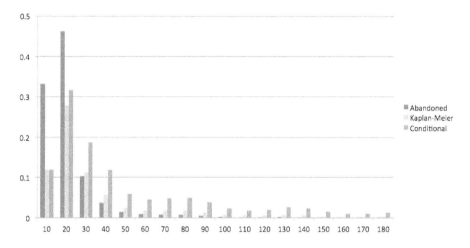

Figure 2.2: Abandonment distributions (in seconds)

When we analyze call-level data then we regularly see the same tele- phone numbers occuring (assuming we have access to this data, of course), also over shorter periods of time. There can be different reasons for that. The first is that callers who abandoned dial again a little later. This what we call a redial. A caller can also dial again after he or she got connected first. There can be, again, multiple reasons for this: either the initial reason of call- ing still exists, or the caller calls for a different issue. The former, which is called a reconnect, is not desirable, the latter usually is. Differentiating be- tween the two is difficult, unless we make a detailed analysis of the contents of the call, or if you have a customer satisfaction survey (which always has missing data and is probably therefore *biased*, because the people participat- ing in a survey are not representative for all customers). A practical solution is that we count all calls that got connected twice within the same day (or couple of hours) as reconnects. Analysis of survey data should validate this

---

The Kaplan-Meier method

The idea behind the Kaplan-Meier method is that connected calls are assumed to have a patience just like the abandoned calls who abandoned after the waiting time of the connected call. For example, if a connected call waited 25 seconds and there are 4 other calls that abandoned after 10, 20, 30 and 40 seconds, then the patience of the connected call could have been 30 or 40, with equal probability. Based on that we derive the overall patience distribution. We assume that a call is equally likely to behave as any one of the calls of which we have data. In the example patience is 10 or 20 with probability 0.2, and 30 or 40 with probability $0.2 + 0.2/2 = 0.3$. See also the table below.

Time	Abandoned/Connected	Kaplan-Meier distribution
10	A	0.2
20	A	0.2
25	C	0
30	A	0.3
40	A	0.3

When there are more connected calls then they should be treated one by one, starting from the ones with the shortest waiting time. Of course 5 calls is by no means enough data to get a reliable patience distribution, usually we need thousands of calls to compute the distribution.

---

approximation. Both redial and reconnect percentages are important PIs.

2.3   Quality of service

We saw that the goal of call center management is to obtain the right tradeoff between costs and quality of service (QoS). We now go into more detail how the QoS can be measured. It consists of several different aspects. Some of these aspects are related to the handling of the calls themselves, such as the way in which the agents attend to the call, and the ratio of calls that need no need further calls, the first-time-fixed or first-call-resolution (FCR) ratio. Others are related to the waiting process, notably the waiting times and the occurrence of abandonments. We focus on waiting times and abandonments, although other aspects of the quality of service can have a large impact on the waiting time and therefore also on the abandonments.

Example   *The help desk of an Internet Service Provider had a considerable rate of callers that phoned back after their call because the answer was not sufficiently clear to solve their problems. By improving scripts and documentation and by additional training this rate was reduced considerable. This not only improved the quality of* *service, it also reduced the number of calls. This had a positive effect on the waiting times, and thus again on the service level.*

Weighted averages

Often we know the SL for short intervals (often giving by the ACD), and we want to compute the SL for longer intervals, for example in a spreadsheet to make a monthly report. The SL of a long period composed of several shorter of which we know the SL can be calculated be averaging in the right way service levels over the shorter periods. When averaging over a number of intervals the number of calls in these intervals should be taken into account. Consider the table below. At first sight the average service level is 75%, by averaging the four percentages, but now the differences in numbers of calls per week are not taken into account.

Week	Number of calls	Answered within 20 s.	SL
1	2000	1900	95%
2	7000	3850	55%
3	5000	3500	70%
4	3000	2400	80%

The right way of calculating is to compute the *fraction* of calls in each interval first. For example, the fraction of calls in the first interval is $\frac{2000}{17000}$, 17000 being the total number of calls over the four weeks. Using these fractions a *weighted average* is calculated in the following way:

$$\frac{2000}{17000} \times 95 + \frac{7000}{17000} \times 55 + \frac{5000}{17000} \times 70 + \frac{3000}{17000} \times 80\% = 68.5\%.$$

This way of calculating averages corresponds to the answer in case the service level was computed directly for the whole month. Indeed, out of a total of 17000 calls 11650 were answered in time, thus a $\frac{11650}{17000} \times 100 = 68.5\%$ service level.

The difference between 68.5 and 75% is not that dramatic. This is because the number of calls in the different weeks are roughly of the same order of magnitude. If the number of calls in the intervals over which we average are very different, then the way of averaging can have an even bigger impact on the result. These big fluctuations typically occur during days. At peak hours we can easily have ten or twenty times as many calls per hour as during the night. Then the difference between ways of averaging can run into the tens of percents.

Weighted averages can easily be computed in Excel. When, in the table above, "Week" is the contents of cell A1, then the weighted average can be computed by the Excel formula =SUMPRODUCT(B2:B5,D2:D5)/SUM(B2:B5). A simpler calculation using the numbers of calls is =SUM(C2:C5)/SUM(B2:B5).

The common way to define quality of service is by looking at the fraction of calls that exceeds a certain waiting time. We call this fraction the *Service Level* (SL). The waiting time that is considered acceptable is known under different names: *Time-to-Answer* (TTA), *Acceptable Waiting Time* (AWT), and *Service Time* (ST) are all used. The "industry standard" is that 80% of all calls should be answered in 20 seconds, but other numbers are possible as well. The SL can simply be calculated as long as there are no abandonments, by dividing the number of calls handled before the AWT by the total number of calls.

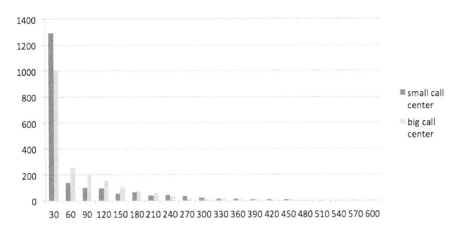

Figure 2.3: Histograms of waiting times (in seconds) for two call centers, with ASA = 60s

The SL is not the only way to measure QoS. Another commonly used waiting time metric is the *average speed of answer* (ASA). This is nothing else than the average over the waiting times. SL and ASA consist of a single number. This is both an advantage and a disadvantage: it is simple, but it gives only limited information. Full information is given by the distribution of the waiting times. Although it is certainly useful to determine this distribution now and then, it does not qualify as PI because of its complexity. The question then becomes: does the SL or the ASA capture the notion of QoS sufficiently? To answer this question we will have a closer look at both. A disadvantage of using the ASA is that the variability is not part of the PI. That is, the ASA does not differentiate between the following two cases: all calls wait exactly 30 seconds, or 90% get connected immediately and 10% waits 300 seconds. In Figure 2.3 we see that the distribution of waiting times for call centers with the same ASA can be quite different. In fact, there is more variability in the waiiting times of the smaller call center.

Thus we look for a simple PI that is sensitive to variability, especially to calls that wait long. An obvious candidate is the SL: it measures the fraction of calls that wait longer than a certain limit. For the SL a similar figure can be made as for the ASA. In Figure 2.4 we plotted the SL for different AWT's for two call centers. An 80/20 SL implies 91/90 for the small call center and 97/90 for the bigger one.

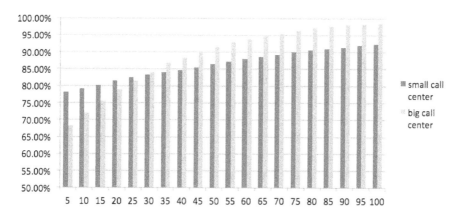

Figure 2.4: SL as function of the AWT (in s) for two call centers with SL = 80%

The disadvantage of the SL is that it not matter how much longer than the AHT a call has waited: it makes no difference between a waiting time of AWT + 1 second and AWT + 100 seconds. A possible solution, that combines ideas from th ASA and the SL, would be the *average excess* (AE): the average time calls have waited beyond the AWT. As an example, if the AWT is 20, and the waiting times are 10, 25, 30 and 25, then the AE is $(0 + 5 + 10 + 5)/4 = 5$ seconds. Despite its disadvantages the SL is the most used PI to represent the waiting time.

The idea of replacing the ASA by the SL is that we avoid long waiting times. However, under an 80/20 SL, 20% of the calls wait longer than the AWT of 20 seconds. To avoid this, we could require a 99/20 SL. However, this requires a much bigger workforce. Is this necessary? This depends on the fact if the caller will accept a long waiting time *now and then*. Consider an individual customer that belongs to the 20% that received bad service. To this customer it is right now irrelevant if the SL was 50/20 or 80/20, in the former case there are just more unsatisfied customers. To the unsatisfied

---

Service orders

In call centers it is customary to serve calls in order of arrival, that is, longest waiting calls first. However, what is the optimal order if we want to minimize the ASA or maximize the SL? For the ASA the order is irrelevant, for the SL it is even better to serve first calls that have not yet exceeded the AWT. In fact, one can argue that calls that have exceeded the AWT should not be served at all: one can better keep the agents available for new arriving calls. Thus steering on SL only pushes call centers to behave in a customer-unfriendly way. This is a reason to avoid penalty clauses in outsourcing contracts based on SL only. Service order is even more relevant in the context of abandonment, which will be treated later on in this chapter.

---

customer the SL becomes relevant when he or she tries to call again. If the SL at that moment is again 80/20, then the probability of another bad experience is 0.2, or 20%. 1 out of 25 customers, 4%, have 2 consecutive bad experiences. And how many customers will try a third time after two bad experiences if they have alternatives? If the competition is strong then offering only an 80/20 SL can lead to churn. Thus whether a 80/20 SL or any other choice is the right SL for a call center depends on the behavior of the callers. Will they call back after a bad experience, and is 20 seconds indeed the correct borderline between good and bad service? Things become even more complicated when we take abandonments into account. See the next section on this subject.

Choices related to SL become also more difficult when we consider call centers with multiple types of calls (see Chapter 6 for more on multi-skill call centers). Consider for example two types of calls for which we like to obtain both an 80/20 SL. Now what if we obtain 70/20 on one and 90/20 on the other? And if we have the choice, with the same means, between 70/20 and 90/20 or 75/20 and 80/20? The former has a better average SL (assuming an equal load), the latter has a higher minimum. The answer depends again on the behavior of callers and the nature of the service: will they mostly generate the same type of call, or do they change type? In the former case we should consider the types independently, in the latter case we should perhaps focus on the average SL.

The situations becomes even more complicated when we have different SL constraints for different call types, for example because we want the sales line to have a better SL than the after-sales line. Here we might have 90/20 and 70/20 constraints, and still be more satisfied when we realize 95/20 and 65/20, simply because we value individual sales calls higher than after-sales calls. A SL definition that corresponds better with our intuitive notion of QoS might consist of a constraint on the high-value calls of 90/20 and an overall constraint over all calls of 80/20.

Example *A call center has two types of calls: calls with a negociated QoS in terms of a SL that has to be met in all situations, and "best effort" traffic where the revenue depends on the QoS. Under high traffic conditions the SL of the first type of calls cannot be met, even when priority is given to these calls. Therefore, the rational decision,* given the contract, *is to give priority to best effort calls in case of high load and to give priority to fixed SL calls when traffic is low to catch up with the SL. This is in complete contradiction with the intentions behind the QoS contract.*

2.4 Abandonments

We saw in Section 2.2 that abandonments are an essential part of customer behavior. In general, abandonments are considered a sign of customer dissatisfaction and should therefore be avoided, even though some calls abandon in less than the AWT. The abandonment rate or percentage is therefore a useful PI for almost any call centers. Usually there is a constraint on the abandonment rate, often in the order of 3 or 5%.

Many call centers combine a constraint on the abandonment rate with a SL constraint. However, we have to decide how abandonments are counted in the SL definition. For this purpose, we classify calls into 4 types. Using the symbol # for the count, this leads to:
- #(connected $\leq$ ATW), the number of calls connected before the AWT;
- #(connected $>$ ATW), the number of calls connected after the AWT;
- #(abandoned $\leq$ ATW), the number of calls abandoned before the AWT;
- #(abandoned $>$ ATW), the number of calls abandoned after the AWT.

The SL is a quotient. The numerator consists of the calls that got good service. In all definitions thus is taken equal to #(connected $\leq$ ATW). More interesting is the denominator. It is clear that all connected calls (#(connected)) should be part of it, but how about the abandoned calls? In practice we find 3 different choices, leading to 3 different SL definitions:

$$\text{SL}_1 = \frac{\#(\text{connected} \leq \text{ATW})}{\#(\text{connected})};$$

$$\text{SL}_2 = \frac{\#(\text{connected} \leq \text{ATW})}{\#(\text{connected}) + \#(\text{abandoned} > \text{ATW})};$$

$$\text{SL}_3 \;=\; \frac{\#(\text{connected} \leq \text{ATW})}{\#(\text{connected}) + \#(\text{abandoned})}.$$

The first definition, SL_1, is sometimes used in combination with the abandonment rate. The big disadvantage is that by not answering calls that have waited more than the AWT the SL can be improved: if a call gets connected in 30 seconds it counts in the denominator, if it abandons it does not count. Thus SL_1 clearly gives a perverse incentive and should not be used for this reason (see, in this context, also the box on page 22).

SL$_2$ and SL$_3$ do not have this disadvantage. Furthermore, it is clear that callers who abandon after the AWT have received bad service, and therefore these calls are added to the number of calls for which the service requirement was not met. For callers that abandon before the AWT it is not that clear. The most reasonable is perhaps not to count these calls at all. This leads to definition SL_2. Counting all abandonments as bad service leads to definition SL_3. Because the numerator increases it is clear that $\text{SL}_1 \geq \text{SL}_2 \geq \text{SL}_3$. That they can be really different is shown in the following example.

Example   *A call center receives 510 calls during an hour. The AWT is set equal to 20 seconds. A total of 460 receive service, of which 410 are answered before 20 seconds. Of the 50 abandoned calls 30 abandon before 20 seconds. The different definitions give:* $\text{SL}_1 = 410/460 = 89\%$, $\text{SL}_2 = 410/480 = 85\%$, *and* $\text{SL}_3 = 410/510 = 80\%$, *a considerable difference.*

These ways of calculating the service level are all easily done on the basis of observed waiting times of calls: one needs to remember the numbers of served and abandoned calls and whether that happens before and after the AWT, in total four numbers per interval for which we want to know the SL.

Virtual waiting time

Another way of defining the service level is to compute it from the waiting time of 'test customers' who have infinite patience. In general this leads to numbers very close to the definition in which we ignore customers who abandon before the AWT. This definition is attractive because it is independent of the patience of a caller. On the other hand, it cannot be observed directly and has to be estimated from the observed statistics. One should have all waiting times (not just the counts) and apply the Kaplan-Meier method (which is explained in the box at page 18) to obtain not the patience distribution but the waiting time distribution. From this the SL can be computed.

We should also consider how to incorporate abandonments in the ASA, in case the ASA is used as service level metric next to or instead of the SL. We can either average over the connected calls or over all calls, or compute the average virtual waiting time using the method explained in the box above.

2.5   Occupancy and shrinkage

In the beginning of this chapter we saw that the service product is characterized by its quality and its costs. In this section we focus on the costs. The majority of the costs in a call center are personnel costs.

Ideally agents should talk to customers 100% of the time they are paid. Unfortunately, this is not the situation, for a number of reasons. Roughly the working time of agents can be divided into two categories: the time that an agent is available to handle calls (or contacts through other channels such as email) and the time an agent cannot take calls. In the former category it can be that the agent is busy with the call (either talking or wrapping up) or that the agent is idle, waiting for a call. In the latter category we find absence because of unforseen situation (such as illness) and holidays, training and coaching, and paid breaks. The fraction of time that the latter category represents is called *shrinkage*. It is an important PI: the lower the shrinkage, the more time agents have for answering calls. On the other hand, a certain amount of shrinkage is unavoidable, because training and coaching are necessary for quality reasons. A shrinkage of 40% is not exceptional.

Next to having a low shrinkage we would like the agents to handle as much contacts as possible while being available for contacts. The indicator for this form of efficiency is the occupancy, measured over a certain period (for example, a week). It is given by:

$$\text{Occupancy} = \frac{\text{Sum of handling times}}{\text{Sum of handling times and total idle time}}.$$

The higher the occupancy, the higher the efficiency. It should be noted however that a occupancy of nearly 100% can only occur for short periods of time, longer periods are too stressful for agents. What a reasonable occupancy target is depends on many factors, including how we count short breaks (are they part of the shrinkage or not?) and the length of the shifts.

Example   *An agent has a contract for 36 hours a week. On average she is absent for 4 hours, she spends 3 hours on training and activities outside the call center, she takes breaks during 230 minutes, she is available waiting for calls during 265 minutes, and she is handling calls (talking plus wrap-up) during 1245 minutes.*

Her occupancy is $1485/(1245 + 265) = 82\%$, if we do not count brakes as part of shrinkage 72%, and if we count all the time she spends at work 58%.

Which definition of PIs is best depends on the situation. If agents are free to take breaks whenever they like then it is probably better to include these in the denominator. In any case, all performance indicator should be considered together: a high occupancy is useless if the FCR percentage is low. In fact, decreasing the first-time-resolution percentage decreases the idle time through an increase in calls and thus "improves" the occupancy.

There are other obvious but interesting relations between the performance indicators. If one tries to decrease the number of performance indicators then one probably ends up considering the number of resolved calls. The disadvantage of this criterion however is that it is hard to measure.

2.6   Further reading

Seddon [32] explains clearly which undesirable outcomes strictly thinking in SLAs can have, with a focus on the health care sector. The example on page 23 comes from the scientific paper Milner & Olsen [22].

Chapter 3

Forecasting

Estimating future workloads is an essential but difficult part of WFM. In this chapter we discuss all aspects of forecasting. We will start with a somewhat technical section about the nature of call arrivals.

3.1 The nature of call arrival processes

To really understand forecasting in call centers we have to understand the nature of call arrival processes, and this goes back to the bahavior of the individual caller. Consider a time interval in a call center, a specific half hour, or perhaps a whole day. Let us say that for this interval the forecast is 100. This means that, out of the perhaps millions of (potential) customers, we predict that 100 will call. Who will call exactly we do not know, but if we have say one million customers, then apparently each has a likelihood of calling of $100/1M = 1/10000$. Thus a forecast (FC) of 100 is equivalent to a probability of calling of $1/10000$ by 1M people. This is all we know about our callers. It is like flipping coins: we know the expected outcome but we never know how many times heads will come up if we try it once. Thus we can never be sure how many people will call, even if we know exactly the likelihood of calling. That is bad news, but the good news is that we do have some quantitative information about the number of people that will call. In the 19th century the French mathematicain Siméon Poisson found that numbers of arrivals follow a certain law, which we now call the *Poisson distribution*. A histogram with 1000 draws from the Poisson distribution with average 100 is shown in Figure 3.1. Actually, the probabaility that precisely 100 arrival will occur is 4%, the probability that the error is bigger

27

than 5% (the outcome is lower than 95 or higher than 105) is 58%. The technically interested reader can reproduce these number with the help of Excel (see the box on page 28).

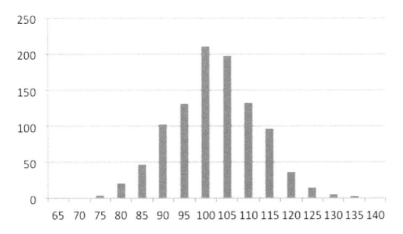

Figure 3.1: Histogram based on the Poisson distribution with average 100

Excel calculations with the Poisson distribution

The Excel Poisson function can be used to calculate Poisson probabilities. It works as follows: if you type = POISSON(30, 35, FALSE) in a cell then you get the probability that there are 30 arrivals when the forecast is 35. Similarly, = POISSON(100, 100, FALSE) gave the 4% mentioned in the text. The "FALSE" refers to the fact that we are only interested in the value 100. To get the probabilities up to a number, we should use "TRUE". Thus = POISSON(94, 100, TRUE) calculates the probability that the outcome is more than 5% lower than the FC 100, around 29%. By calculating = POISSON(105, 100, TRUE) we get the probability that the outcome is lower than or equal to 105, around 71%. Then the probability that the outcome is higher than 105, that is, more than 5% higher than the FC, is 29%. By adding both probabilities we get the probability that the error is more than 5%: 58%.

In case you use a non-English version of Excel you can look up the name of the Poisson function by searching the functions for "poisson" or by searching the internet for a table with translations.

The high variability of the Poisson distribution might come as a surprise: when the FC is 100, then only because of "natural" variability there is an 58% probability that the error is higher than 5%. In many call centers this is not acceptable. Luckily, the percentage error, that is, the error relative to the value, decreases with the value of the forecast. As an example, consider a FC of 1000. The probability that the error is more than 5% is now only 11%, and for a FC of 10000 it is negligable, smaller than a millionth.

Variability of the Poisson distribution

Understanding of this box requires familiarity with the normal distribution. In Figure 3.1 we see that the Poisson distribution looks much like a normal distribution, we recognize the bell shape. In fact, the Poisson distribution is well approximated by a normal distribution, rounded to the nearest integer, with mean $\mu = $ FC and standard deviation $\sigma = \sqrt{FC}$. Thus the standard deviation increases with FC, but decreases relative to FC, because $FC/\sqrt{FC}$ is a decreasing function of FC.

For the variability of the normal distribution we have the following rule of thumb: the probability that the deviation from the mean is bigger than the standard deviation is around 32%. Translated to the Poisson distribution this gives: the probability that the deviation from the FC is bigger than the square root of the FC is around 32%. As an example, take FC = 1000. The probability that the outcome is more than 31 higher or lower than 1000 (a 3% error) is approximately 32%.

Let us translate these results to the practice of forecasting. We see that, even starting from a perfect forecast, there is a considerable "natural" Poisson variability. Next to that, there are errors in the forecast. These errors can be small or big, but always exist. One of the challenges in forecasting is to find the reason of the differences between actuals and FC. Forecasting errors scale with the volume: when the volume is twice as high, then the error is twice as big. The Poisson error increases less quickly: when the volume is twice as high, then the Poisson error is $\sqrt{2} \approx 1.4$ times as big (see the box "variability of the Poisson distribution"). Thus, the higher the volume, the easier it is to attribute errors to the FC, and the easier it is to "explain" the errors. For this reason it is better to forecast at an aggregated level, at days or weeks.

Example *The forecast for a certain day was 1200. For the 14 hours the call center was open the FC ranged from around 45 to 140. At the hour level the error was around 10 to 15, and sometimes above and sometimes below the FC. At the day level the actual was 1280, which is very unlikely to be caused solely by Poisson fluctuations: the probability of an outcome of 1280 or higher for a Poisson distribution with mean 1200 is 1%.*

Arrival experiment

An interesting Excel experiment which helps us develop our understanding of arrival processes is as follows. Imagine a very small B2B call center with 20 customers that each call with a 15% probability. Let us simulate in Excel one "actual". By entering $=$ IF(RAND() $< 0.15, 1, 0$) we generate a 1 with probability 15%. By copying this formula 19 times and summing the outcomes we can simulate a single day. By pushing F9 (recalculate) we simulate new days. By copying the whole simulation multiple times we get simulations of multiple days next to each other. Of this we can make a histogram. The lefthand bars in the figure below are an example. The righthand bars are the Poisson distribution with average 3. (For the mathematically interested: the "real" distribution for such a small population (20) is the binomial distribution. It is very close to the Poisson, which is exact when the population gets big and the contact probability small. See also the box on page 117.)

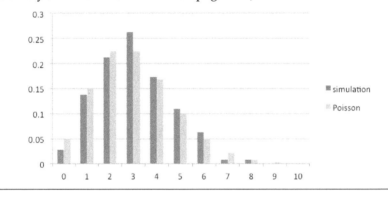

3.2 The goal of forecasting

We saw that forecasts are always "wrong": actuals always deviate from forecasts. The goal of forecasting is to make forecasts that are as accurate as possible, i.e., as close to the actuals as possible. This requires a special attitude towards forecasting in which we try to learn from our errors and are always busy improving the forecasting process. This is a systematic data-driven approach, in which we let the numbers decide which way of forecasting is best. Thus it is important to specify what a good forecast is and when one forecast is better than the other.

The difference between the forecast and actual is called the error. The quality of a forecast can never be judged from a single error: it can be completely coincidental that the error is big or small. We always have to consider multiple intervals, for example days of the week. Taking intervals that are too small is neither a good idea: then the Poisson variability is dominating the errors. There are multiple ways to translate errors by interval into one overall number. They have names such as *mean squared error* and *mean absolute error*. We focus on the MAPE and the WAPE, the *mean* and *weighted absolute percentage error*. We introduce some mathematical notation to define them. Afterwards we give an example.

Assume that we consider n intervals, and let FC_i be the forecast in the ith time interval. We assume that A_i is the actual in interval i. Then the difference $A_i - FC_i$ is the error. Dividing by the actual leads to the percentage error: $(A_i - FC_i)/A_i$. Omitting the sign when the number is negative gives the absolute percentage error: $|(A_i - FC_i)/A_i|$. Averaging over the periods leads finally to the MAPE:

$$\frac{1}{n}\sum_{i=1}^{n}\left|\frac{A_i - FC_i}{A_i}\right|.$$

Example *In the table below forecasts, actuals and further calculations for the days of a certain week are given. The MAPE, the average over the last column, is 13.2%.*

forecasts FC_i	actuals A_i	errors $A_i - FC_i$	percentage errors $\frac{A_i - FC_i}{A_i}$	absolute percentage errors $\left|\frac{A_i - FC_i}{A_i}\right|$
320	286	-34	-12%	12%
300	302	2	1%	1%
300	259	-41	-16%	16%
300	297	-3	-1%	1%
280	270	-10	-4%	4%
50	53	3	6%	6%
20	13	-7	-54%	54%

The disadvantage of the MAPE is immediately clear from the example: a big percentage error for a small actual can cause a big MAPE. In the example, the bad result for the last day explains more than half of the MAPE. The WAPE is an answer to that: high-volume days are counted heavier than low-volume days. Without further explanation we give the WAPE:

$$\frac{\sum_{i=1}^{n}|A_i - FC_i|}{\sum_{i=1}^{n}A_i}.$$

The WAPE of the example is 6.8%.

Division by 0

We saw that small actuals can cause a high MAPE. Driven to the extreme, it might occur that an actual is 0, for example if we measure actuals every 15 minutes during low-volume periods such as during the night. In that case, we divide by 0 and the MAPE becomes infinite. For this reason the MAPE is inappropriate for this type of situation. Instead one should use the WAPE or yet other measures such as the *SMAPE*.

Looking at (weighted) averages of errors has the same disadvantage as the ASA: it does not measure the variability in the errors. An alternative, which is simple and takes variability into account to a certain extent, measures to which extend the error is for example below 5%. Note the parallel with the SL. In the example the error is below 5% in 57% of the cases.

The MSE

Another measure that is often used is the Mean Squared Error (MSE). It is calculated by multiplying all errors with themselves and then taking the average. In the example this leads to a MSE of $((-34)^2 + 2^2 + \cdots + (-7)^2)/7 = 429.7$. It is a disadvantage that this number is hard to interpret. The MSE is very sensitive to big errors. Big fluctuations in actuals are usually due to special events for which separate procedures exist. Thus they should not influence the KPI for forecasting accuracy too much. For this reason the MSE is less appropiate than the MAPE or the WAPE for forecasting.

Forecasting is not a goal by itself, forecasts are used to make decisions of different types. Short-term forecasts, expanding over several weeks are mainly used for workforce management. Mid-term forecasts, in the range of months, are used for human resource decisions related to hiring and training. Long-term forecasts, in the range of years, are used for strategic and financial decisions. The granularity of the forecast is different depending on the horizon: long-term forecasts are at the month or even at the quarter or year level, while short-term forecasts used in WFM require forecasts at the interval level. On an even shorter horizon we have intra-day adaptations based on the first part of the day, which is useful for intra-day performance management.

Because of the higher aggregation level long-term horizon forecasting is less influenced by Poisson fluctuation, in that sense it is easier. However, long-term volume is influenced by so-called "trend" changes, for example due to changes in the economic situation or competition. Therefore long-term forecasts are often much less accurate than short-term forecasts, and will often be systematically higher or lower than the actuals (see page 50 for more on this).

For a number of reasons, of which the influence of the Poisson error is one, it is usually better to separate intra-day forecasting into forecasting of daily volumes and the determination of profiles which are used to distribute the daily volume over the intervals of the day. On the next pages we will concentrate on forecasting at the level of days, weeks and months. On page 46 we discuss how to use day-level forecast and profiles to produce intra-day forecasts.

3.3 The building blocks

There are roughly speaking three approaches to forecasting: using a tool in which advanced mathematical forecasting methods are implemented, using a simpler but systematic approach that is executed by the forecaster, and using a non-systematic approach largely based on human judgment. Generally speaking, simple mathematical methods outperform both more sophisticated methods and human judgment. One of the problems with pure human judgment is that it lacks objectivity. Humans tend to show wishful thinking. For example, when sales are lagging behind target then one is tempted to overestimate call volume on the sales line. Next to that, it is often hard to explain fluctuations in call volume: fluctuations can have multiple causes, each having an unclear impact. This lack of a clear relation between cause and effect makes it for humans hard to understand. Finally, it takes long before our judgments are tested, because forecasting is done days in advance. That makes learning slow. For all these reasons forecasting purely on human judgments should be avoided. On the other hand, relying completely on a computerized system won't work either: every forecasting method must rely on human interaction to identify special events, interpret system changes, and so forth. This human interaction, characteristic for *decision support systems*, makes it important that forecasters understand the consequences of their interaction with the system. This disqualifies some of the more advanced black box-type forecasting methods for practical use. For these reasons we focus on a systematic approach based on relatively simple mathematical methods.

Daily actuals are influenced by a number of factors in addition to the

Poisson fluctuations. These factors are:

- **Seasonality**, the fact that certain increases and decreases in traffic occur each year around the same time. To measure seasonality we need at least two years of data;
- **Holidays**, the fact that certain fluctuations are caused by holidays such as Easter and Christmas;
- **Day of the week**, the fact that there is also a form of seasonality at the weekly level;
- **Actions & special events**, such as marketing events, unusual weather conditions, but also technical issues in the call center that influence (the registration of) the number of calls;
- **Trend**, long-term fluctuations that do not repeat themselves every year.

To be able to predict the future we need to understand what has happened in the past and extrapolate that to the future. Thus analyzing the historic volume and explaining what has happened using the factors above is perhaps the most important part of forecasting. Because we will analyze the influence of these factors one by one these methods are known as *decomposition* methods. Let us first summarize how it is done. Then we explain the different steps in detail.

Every statistical analysis starts with plotting the data to get an overall impression. However, making a graphical plot of the actuals for the time we have data on is often little insightful: the weekly cycle and the special events might well obscure the identification of for example a slight but steady increase in call volume. A typical example is Figure 3.2: we clearly see the weekly effect, with less traffic on Saterday. The Sundays, with no traffic at all, are left out. We also see some outliers, on January 1, and towards the end of the graph. However, from the graph it is hard to say if we identified all outliers and an eventual trend. For this reason, we have to identify the special events and holidays as far as we can and then *deseasonalize* the data. This should be done for the weekly cycle, but also for the yearly cycle if enough data is available. In the ideal situation we get a straight line when special days and the seasons are filtered out. This straight line represents the long-term trend. Of course, when it is flat, then there is no trend. However, we rarely get such a straight line, there are still unexplained variations. Part of these are due to the Poisson fluctuations, but often they are bigger than we would expect just from the Poisson distribution. Forecasting methods exist to identify the trend in the presence of these fluctuations. That finishes the analysis of the historical data, and we start the actual forecasting. First we extrapolate the trend to the future, as many days as we need to forecast. After that we seasonalize the data. A special treatment is reserved for the special events and holidays: based on estimations of their historic impact we forecast future special days.

In the next section we study deseasonalizing in detail.

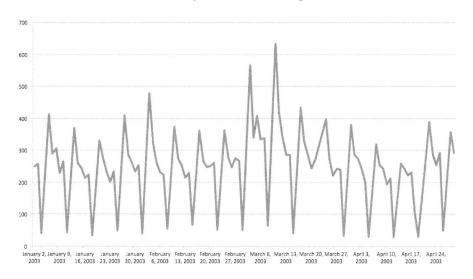

Figure 3.2: Daily volume for a call center showing the weekly pattern and some outliers

3.4 Deseasonalizing

In daily call center data there are usually two seasons, the weeks and the years. Taking out the intra-week pattern is done as follows. Calculate first the average per day of the week over a longer period, leaving out the special days. Then determine the proportion for each day of week. Now we take out the intra-week effect by dividing the volume of every day by the factor belonging to that day. What remains is data with less fluctuations and the special days sticking out. When the call center is closed a fixed day or days of the week it is better to eliminate these days from the data instead of using 0s, as we did with the Sundays in Figure 3.2. Applied to this numbers (which spans several years) shows for example an average Monday volume of 542.7 and an average Sunday volume of 62.7. Figure 3.3 shows the volume divided by the daily averages. We see a number of things. There are

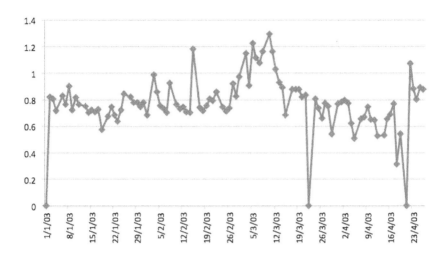

Figure 3.3: Daily volume with intra-week pattern filtered out

3 days with no volume at all, they are indeed holidays. February 15, a Saturday, clearly sticks out. Furthermore, we see a steady rise and decline of volume. To decide whether that is trend or seasonality we have to look at more data.

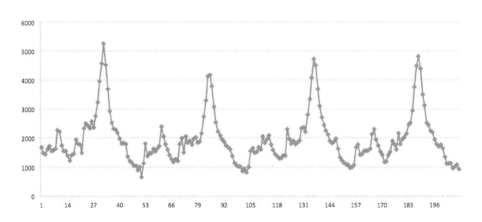

Figure 3.4: Weekly volume over 4 years showing the seasonal pattern

In Figure 3.4 we plotted the weekly volume for 4 consecutive years. We see a very clear cyclical effect, with a peak in the middle of each year, but also some smaller regularities seem to be present. They become clearer when we plot the 4 years on top of each other as in Figure 3.5. We can now filter out the seasonal pattern, much as we filtered out the weekly pattern: we divide the volume in every week by the average volume of that week over all years. This leads to Figure 3.6.

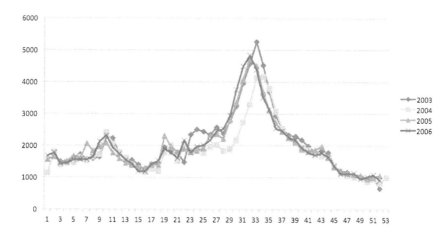

Figure 3.5: Weekly volume of 4 years showing the same seasonal pattern

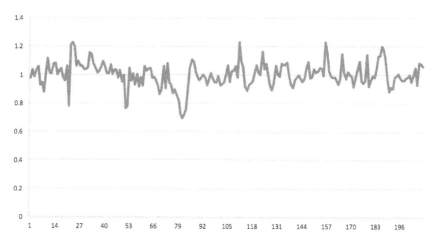

Figure 3.6: Weekly volume after elimination of the yearly pattern

Ideally, Figure 3.6 would be a straight line without any fluctuations. Although the line is quite flat (more than 50% of the points lie within the [0.95,1.05] interval), there are some outliers, some even lower than 0.8 or bigger than 1.2. The first 4 outliers are weeks 22–25 in the first year. Their

---

Different methods for deseasonalizing

A somewhat different method for deseasonalizing is as follows. Consider first for every week the proportion of volume of that week compared to the whole year, and then average these proportions over a number of years. If this method is better than the one described in the text depends on the situation; the advantage of the first method is that it can also be used if you have incomplete data over certain years.

---

difference compared to the other years can to some extent be explained by the days at which Ascension and Pentecost fall: the first low week contains Ascension which is often low, the week after is usually higher, but there seems to be no reason for the next two week with high volume. Also in Figure 3.5 they clearly stick out. The next outliers are around the end of the first year. They have to do with the fact that Christmas and New Year's Day not always fall on the same day nor in the same week. For the next outliers in the summer of 2004 there is no explanation based on Holidays. In fact, this is the only place where the line is low for a considerable number of successive weeks, unless we count the weeks around week 185, the summer of the last year. Part of this is due to the low around week 81, the summer of the second year: they make the other summers stick out higher. This is precisely why exceptional days and weeks should not be considered when deseasonalizing. For known exceptions such as holidays this is easily done, but for outliers which are discovered after deseasonalizing this leads to a cyclical procedure in which the deseasonalization and forecasting is done at least twice. It can be hard to decide what is an outlier and what isn't. A clear definition is required, for example an error with respect to the forecasted value of more than 20%.

Week numbers

In the situation of considerable intra-year fluctuations it is important to match corresponding weeks in different years in the right way. This match is not necessarily based on the week numbers: it might be better to match holiday calendars. In fact, the Dutch summer holidays in 2005 and 2006 started one week earlier than in 2003 and 2004, explaining the shift in peak in Figure 3.6. Taking this into account improves the quality of the forecast.

It is also worth noting that the week numbers in MS Excel, given by the WEEKNUM() function, differ from the ISO standard. According to ISO, week 1 is the first week with four or more of its days in the starting year. The Excel week number function counts the week with January 1 in it as week 1. On the internet one can find solutions to use the ISO numbering in Excel.

> **Forecasting at month level**
> In certain situations, for example for long-term hiring or financial reasons, we might prefer to forecast at the monthly level. However, the disadvantage of forecasting at the month level is that the number of working days in a month varies, also for the same month in different years. For example, March 2010 counted 23 working days, while March 2009 counted only 21 (of which Easter Monday was one), simply because March 1 was a Saturday. If we do not correct for this we introduce fluctuations by forecasting at the month level. Several methods for correcting this effect exist, also depending on the weekend volume in the call center. An alternative might be to forecast at the quarter (13 week) level, or to forecast periods with, successively, 4, 4 and 5 weeks.

3.5 Mathematical forecasting methods

Short-term fluctuations in call centers are mostly due to intra-week variations, special days, and seasonal fluctuations. The trend plays a lesser role. For this reason short-term forecasting, as we use for WFM, is mostly influenced by the seasonal patterns and exceptions. Trend is of some importance, but becomes crucial when we consider long-term forecasting.

The simplest forecasting method, without taking the trend into account, consists of taking the average over the last data points. The forecast will consists of a straight line at the level of this average. Thus, the average is used as the *fit* for the actuals and then it is extrapolated to the future to form the forecast: see Figure 3.7. The average in this situation is 1103.05. Note it is not a real number. Rounding does not make a big difference, but note that in general a forecast need not be an integer.

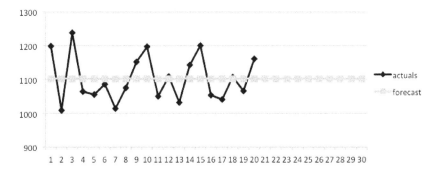

Figure 3.7: Actuals with a fit and forecast using the average

An important question is how many data points to take: if we take too many data points then irrelevant outdated data is used; if we take not enough data points then irrelevant fluctuations, such as the Poisson "noise", influence the average. Usually we take a fixed number of data points, for example 20 weeks. Whether this number should be 5, 20 or 50 depends on the data series. As time progresses new data become available and old data is discarded because we take a fixed number of data points. For this reason this number is called a *moving average*. Instead of a moving average we can also take the median. The advantage of the median over the average is that it is less sensitive to outliers, but which one is best should be determined by the numbers. In Figure 3.8 we see the last deseasonalized actuals of Figure 3.6, and the 1-week forecast based on a median with data of 35 weeks back, and a moving average (MA) based on 10 weeks of data. Experimenting with different numbers showed that the median(35) has the lowest WAPE, of 5.6%. The number 10 was chosen arbitrarily; MA(10) has a WAPE of 6.6%. In fact, the WAPEs of all medians and moving averages vary little with the number of data points, they do not exceed 7%.

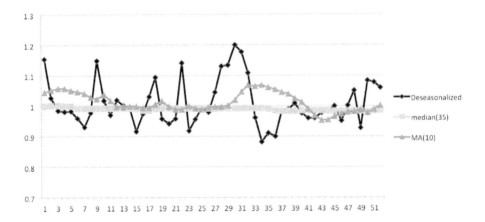

Figure 3.8: Deseasonalized weekly volume and moving average and median forecasts

In many situations the forecast can be improved by including a trend. Sometimes, especially in long-term forecasting, this is even the essence of forecasting. The average and the median can be generalized to what is known as linear regression (LR) and quantile regression, respectively. We will start by discussing linear regression. Books exist that are entirely de-

> **Average versus median**
>
> For a given set of actuals, the average is the number that minimizes the *mean squared error* (see the box on page 32). The median is the number that minimizes the WAPE. Thus, if we try to *fit* a horizontal line that minimizes the WAPE for a certain set of actuals, then we should choose the median as its value. This does not mean that the median always gives the best *forecast*. This is only true under certain mathematical conditions that are usually not satisfied for call center actuals. And even in such a situation it is only true in a statistical sense: when repeated many times the average WAPE will be lower for the median, but for any separate forecasting problem nothing can be said.

voted to linear regression; we only discuss the basic concepts that are relevant to forecasting. Linear regression in its simplest form consists of replacing the horizontal line of Figure 3.7 by a line that is not necessary horizontal, but that also has a slope. It consists of finding the straight line that follows the data best (in the sense that it minimizes the mean squared error: see the box on page 41). Many software packages have the ability to execute LR. This holds also for Excel. Using the functions SLOPE() and INTERCEPT() we can find the intercept with the vertical axis and the slope.

Example   *Consider a forecasting problem with 10 actuals as in the figure. Using INTERCEPT(B2:K2,B1:K1) and SLOPE(B2:K2,B1:K1) we determine the slope and intercept of the linear regression. The forecast is then constructed by taking the intercept plus the time times the slope. Thus M4 is equal to B3+M1∗E3.*

In Figure 3.9 we see 4 years of weekly actuals, before and after deseasonalizing, of a call center. We see a trend that is increasing in the first year and slowly decreasing afterwards (the left axis is for the actuals, the right axis for the deseasonalized data).

Let us use LR to approximate the trend. An important question is how many data points to take. In Figure 3.10 we plotted the last year of the deseasonalized data of plus 3 linear regressions, based on all data, the last year, and the last 10 weeks. We clearly see the importance of the amount of data used: at the first forecasted week the difference between the highest and the lowest FC is more than 6%, and it increases to 17% at the end of the forecasted year.

Many different forecasting methods exist. Linear regression (which is in

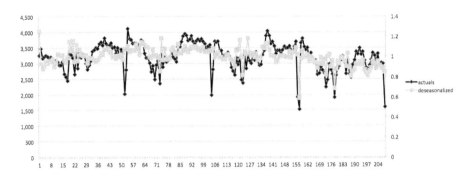

Figure 3.9: Four years of weekly actuals and deseasonalized actuals of a call center

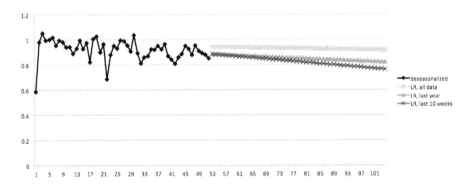

Figure 3.10: One year of deseasonalized weekly volume and three LR forecasts

essence not a forecasting method, but a method to relate response variables to explanatory variables, in our situation actuals and time) is by far the most studied, but not necessarily the best. Given its relation to the WAPE (see the box on page 32) quantile regression is a logical candidate, but it is actually one of the least used methods. It is technically rather involved; more details are given in the box "quantile regression".

Another often used class of mathematical forecasting methods are so-called *smoothing methods*. The idea behind smoothing is that most recent is most important for forecasting and should have the highest *weight*; the older the data, the lower the weight. Similar to what we discussed thus far we have a simple method to find a constant forecast and linear forecasts.

Up to now we discussed constant and linear forecasts. This often suffices to make good forecasts, especially for short-term forecasting as is needed for WFM. However, for long-term forecasting linear forecasts are sometimes

> ### Quantile regression
> The objective of quantile regression is to find the straight line that minimizes the sum of absolute errors. Assume that the actual at time t_i is given by A_i. The fit F_i is given by $a + bt_i$: this a is the intercept and b is the slope. The goal is to find a and b such that $\sum_i |E_i|$ is minimized where E_i is the error at t_i: $E_i = A_i - F_i$. Using a trick we can write this problem as a linear optimization problem, a class of problems which we will discuss in detail in Chapter 5. The trick is as follows: we can write E_i as $E_i^+ - E_i^-$, where E_i^+ and E_i^- are both positive, the positive and negative parts of the error. Then the objective becomes a linear function: $\sum_i (E_i^+ - E_i^-)$. Turning the fit into a forecast using the intercept a and the slope b is done in exactly the same way as in LR.

not the best choice. It might even give strange results. To illustrate this, look at some more volatile call center actuals, as in Figure 3.11, both from the same call center. A linear regression would give in one case a forecast that grows without bound; in the other case it would mean that the forecast eventually becomes negative. It is evident that this is impossible, and a more advanced forecasting method is required.

Different methods exist to avoid the linear forecasts. We could try to fit a non-linear function which eventually stabilizes. In fact, we could generalize LR to allow for mutiple, non-linear functions.

Another method is applying a transformation first. A good example is taking a logarithm of the actuals. Then we do the complete forecasting with the transformed data, and in the end we transform back using the exponential function. This guarantees that the FC is always positive; however, it can still easily grow to infinity. A group of advanced mathematical forecasting methods exist called ARIMA models. Here it is possible to model cyclical effects of a certain number of actuals. However, for these methods to determine all parameters enough actuals including multiple cycles are needed, data which is rarely available in call centers. This, together with the black box nature of the methods, make them less suitable for call center forecasting.

3.6 Constructing the forecast

Once the trend is determined we have to include the seasons (intra-week and intra-year) first and then the special days to produce the forecast. While deseasonalizing consisted of dividing by the average per day or week, seasonalizing consists of multiplying the deseasonalized FC by the seasonal factors. For the LRs of Figure 3.10 this leads to the FCs in Figure 3.12.

To correct the forecast for special days and events we have to quantify first their effect. To do this we need data on at least one but preferably more occurences of each event. For certain events, especially those where the day of the week changes such as Christmas, this is not always the case. When we have one or more events then we can determine its impact, possibly by averaging. Later on we can include this impact in the forecast.

Smoothing methods

The simplest smoothing method is called exponential smoothing. All it takes is a constant, often the greek letter α is taken. Now, when a new actual A is known the last forecast value FC is taken and the new forecast becomes $\alpha * A + (1 - \alpha) * FC$. The figure shows how this can be implemented in Excel.

	A	B	C	D	E	F
1	day	actual	FC		smoothing parameter	
2					0.3	
3	1	332	280.0			
4	2	336	295.6			
5	3	344	307.7			
6	4	300	318.6			
7	5	353	313.0			
8	6	385	325.0			
9	7	332	343.0			
10	8	398	339.7			
11	9	370	=E2*B10+(1-E2)*C10			
12	10	401	361.0			
13	11	399	373.0			
14	12	425	380.8			
15	13	368	394.1			
16	14	409	386.3			
17	15	345	393.1			
18	16	427	378.7			
19	17	442	393.2			
20	18	476	407.8			
21	19	406	428.3			
22	20	396	421.6			
23						

Exponential smoothing gives a constant forecast, just as a moving average. A trend can also be included in the smoothing algorithm: now there two constant that are estimated by smoothing, both the level and the slope. This method is known as Holt's method, which is thus an alternative for linear regression. It is our experience that often LR gives better results than smoothing due to the relative importance given to the last actuals.

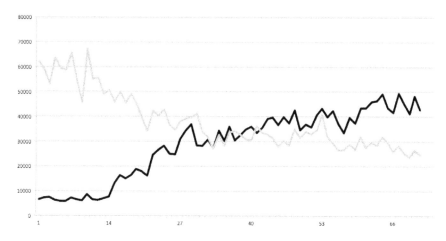

Figure 3.11: Highly volatile monthly actuals

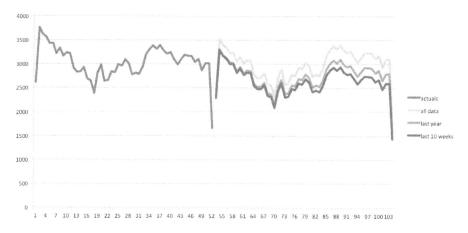

Figure 3.12: Actuals and three forecasts based on linear regression

Example   *We analyze a call center that is closed on Easter Monday. For week 2 to 16 we calculated the fraction of volume on every weekday for 2 years consecutive years. In the figures below we see the week of Easter, the minimum and the maximum over the other weeks and the median. We clearly see that the Easter weeks are very much alike and very different from the other weeks.*

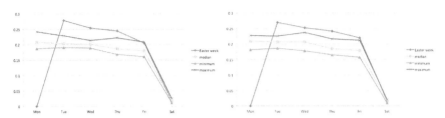

Now we take the weekly factors, for example the median, and we modify that in the following way: Easter Monday has factor 0, and the Tuesday get 10% extra volume, that is, its factor is multiplied by 1.1. The factors for Wednesday to Saturday remain the same. Then we normalize the factors making sure they sum up to 1. The resulting profiles are depicted in the following figure. The fit is excellent, although the statistical evidence is weak because it is only based on two occurences.

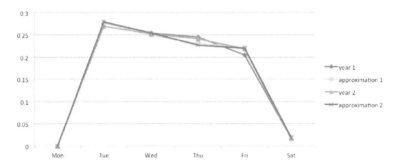

3.7   Intra-day forecasts

Up to now we forecasted the daily volume. For WFM we need forecasts at the 15 or 30-minute level, the level at which the workforce scheduling is done. In many call centers the volume, especially outside the busiest hours, is so low that the Poisson variability plays an important role. And it is not the Poisson variability that we are interested in, but the underlying expected volume, the average value of the Poisson distribution, as discussed in Section 3.1. To estimate this average, we need multiple actuals, one day of actuals will not suffice to give a good intra-day profile.

Example   *A call center is open 24 hours a day for emergencies, but receives few calls in the nightly hours. The volume on a particular night, between 1am and 5am, ranges from 0 to 6. Staffing levels based on this single night, using the Erlang C formula (with an AHT of 5 minutes and a 80/20 SL) range from 0 to 4. Evidently,* *these staffing levels, and the underlying forecasts, are completely determined by the randomness of the Poisson process. Averaging over multiple nights leads to a forecasts of little over 2 for all quarters, and a constant staffing level of 2.*

The risk of taking an average over many days is that the information that is used is outdated. With intra-day profiles this is usually not the case. Of course, there are call centers with seasonal changes in intra-day profiles, but most often these profiles only change little over time (but they are different for different days of the week). Averaging over multiple week leads leads to accurate intra-day profiles, but also to *smooth* profiles. A good profile is expected to be smooth: there are no reasons to expect spikes at certain times of the day, we expect the volume to change gradually. Exceptions are lines where suddenly the routing of calls is changed (for example, when a third party takes over all traffic after office hours). Thus a smooth profile is a sign of sufficient averaging, but it also makes efficient staffing possible: spikes in forecasts will lead to inefficient planning by the WFM tool, and to a bad SL because the agents are scheduled at the wrong moments.

In Figure 3.13 we plotted intra-day forecasts for a call center using profiles which are based on different numbers of days. The more days we take, the smoother the forecast. The greatest differences occur during the busiest moments, but percentagewise, the greatest differences can be found during the night. Actually, for some quarters the actuals are 0, and because of this some absolute percentage errors, and also the MAPE, become infinite (see the box on page 32).

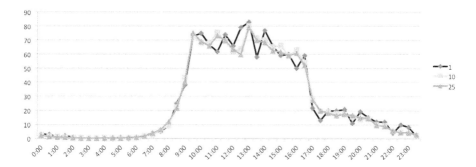

Figure 3.13: Intra-day forecasts using profiles based on different numbers of days

In Table 3.1 we see the results for a single representative day for different intra-day profiles and a daily forecast of 1278 which is accurate. While the error on the daily volume is small, we see that the WAPE is very big, and bigger for profiles based on less weeks. The errors for the profile based on 25 weeks is almost entirely due to the Poisson noise of the actuals. The errors for the profile based on 1 week are on one side due to the Poisson noise, but equally to the forecasting error because we have a profile based on a single day. Incidentally the errors cancel out, that is why the WAPE is not twice as big as for the case with 25 weeks.

# of weeks in profile	25	10	1
WAPE	14.2%	14.6%	18.7%
% that AE > 10%	56.8%	67.6%	70.3%
overall APE	2.2%	3.8%	4.2%

Table 3.1: Performance for different intra-day profiles

An important question that remains is how many weeks to use for the averaging. From the discussion so far it must be clear that this depends on the volume, and thus also on the time of day we are mostly interested in. If we want to obtain a certain precision for all intervals we should look at the interval with the lowest volume, but perhaps our requirements on these intervals are less restrictive than for busy intervals. If we want to obtain an error lower than 5% in at least 96% of the cases then we need at least 1600 calls in all weeks together; if an error of 5% or higher in at most 68% of the cases suffices, then we need 400 calls. Details of the calculation can be found in the box below. Note that this calculation is done per interval, to obtain the required precision we should have these numbers of actuals in all intervals. Note as well that these numbers are needed to deal with the Poisson noise. To deal with other sources of fluctuations it can be the case that we need considerably more days to determine accurate intra-day profiles. The numbers given here are the minima; by looking at the smoothness of a profile we can judge whether we have averaged over enough days.

3.8   The forecasting process

Up to now we described the standard approach to call center forecasting. However, it is not a standard recipe; many choices have to be made, and the correct answers depend on the specifications of the forecasting problem. Aspects that might differ from one call center to the next are the objective, the amount of available data, the volatility, the extend to which special days

---

Averaging daily profiles

To compute the total number of actuals required to obtain a certain precision of an intra-day forecast we should first realize that this precision can only be obtained in a statistical way. To derive such a statistical statement, we use the fact that the total number of actuals in a certain interval, summed over multiple weeks, has again a Poisson distribution. Furthermore, this Poisson distribution looks very much like a normal distribution. For the normal distribution we have the following rule of thumb: 68.2% (95.8%) of all outcomes lie within 1 (2) standard deviation from the mean. See the figure below (taken from Wikipedia) for an illustration of this rule.

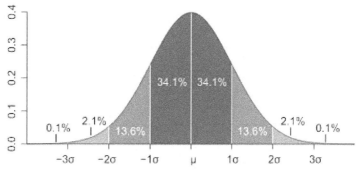

What is the precision when one averages over n profiles? The actual, coming from a Poisson distribution, has a standard deviation of $\sqrt{FC}$. Statistical theory tells that an average over n profiles has standard deviation $\sqrt{FC/n}$. To get, say, an error that is with 95.8% probability not bigger than 5%, we need that $2\sqrt{FC/n} \leq 0.05FC$. The minimal n for which this is the case is $n \approx 1600/FC$.

---

play a role, and so forth. The only way to decide what the best choices are is to test them in practice. What is best might change over time. Therefore the forecasters are regularly busy updating the forecasting method. Only this way it is possible to produce high-quality forecasts.

In practice we see that few call centers adopt a systematic approach of continuous improvement. Short-term obligations often dominate the agendas of planners and forecasters giving them little time to think more fundamentally about the forecasting process. Furthermore, management is often not aware of the possible gains of such an exercise. Finally, forecasters often lack the knowledge to think more fundamentally about their forecasting procedure. It might be necessary to involve business analysts with a stronger (scientific) background in mathematics and forecasting.

Such a systematic approach to forecasting involves analyzing errors, determining trend changes and trying out other forecasting methods to see if,

---

PDCA

An often used management method for continuous improvement is known under the acronym PDCA, *plan-do-check-act*. It is also known as the Deming wheel, after the statistician Deming. It is part of lean management, and has a place in quality norms such as COPC and ISO 9001.

---

with hindsight, they would have performed better. Of course, if incidentally another method performs better this is not a reason to adopt it immediately. On the other hand, when a different method for some time consistently performs better then this might be a reason to change method. Note that we could evaluate different methods because we did not use all data for constructing a forecast; we used less data to be able to produce a forecast for the most recent period. Sometimes the first period is called the *training set* and the most recent data the *test set*. This is also a good way to set up the method initially. Sufficient data is a requirement to use this method. If we do not have enough data then we determine the best fit, but it is not always true that the best fit also gives the best forecast.

3.9   Statistical forecast bounds

Forecasting as we discussed it so far consists of formulating a best guess of the volume in a number of intervals, knowing that there is always an error, which we wish to minimize. In the box on page 49 we quantified this error for the Poisson noise. We created bounds between which the actual will be, with a certain likelihood. This idea could be generalized to forecasting in general: instead, or next to the regular forecast we could compute upper and lower bounds which represent for each interval a range between which the actual falls with a certain likelihood. An example of such a forecast is given in Figure 3.14.

The numbers in Figure 3.14 are calculated as follows. To estimate the accuracy of our forecasting procedure we calculated the 10-week forecast for periods for which we already know the actuals. In this way we could evaluate the precision. We did this repeatedly to obtain a certain statistical precision, and to be able to estimate in this situation the 10 and 90% precision of the forecast. To understand that we should look at Figure 3.15. It shows the errors of 50 consecutive 1-week ahead forecasts. The average error is close to 0%: there is no systematic forecasting error. We see in the figure that 10% of the percentage errors are −7% or lower, and 10% are 9% or

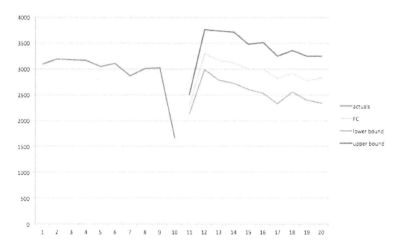

Figure 3.14: 10 and 90% bounds for weekly forecasts

higher. Thus the bounds to the 1-week ahead forecast are the forecast minus 7% and plus 9%. This is exactly how the bounds is week 11 are constructed: the FC is 2293, the lower bound is $2293 \times 93\% \approx 2132$, the upper bound is $2293 \times 109\% \approx 2503$. (When you check these calculations you will find small differences: they are explained by the fact that 7 and 9 are rounded percentages.)

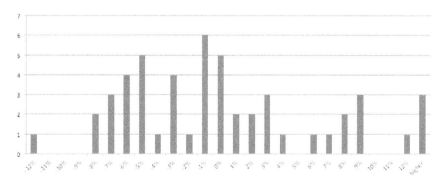

Figure 3.15: Histogram with errors of 51 consecutive 1-week ahead forecasts

Note that many people with some statistical background would use the normal distribution to compute bounds. In the box on page 52 it is explained why this is not a good idea.

The bounds for the 2 upto 10-week forecasts are calculated in much the

---

Using the normal distribution

A tempting (but erroneous!) alternative approach to estimate the bounds would be as follows. From the percentage errors we could derive the standard deviation (0.01 for the 1-week FC in the example) and then use a normal approximation to find the 10 and 90% quantiles of the error. However, here we assume implicitly that the errors look like a normal distribution, and that is in general not the case, as is illustrated in the figure below.

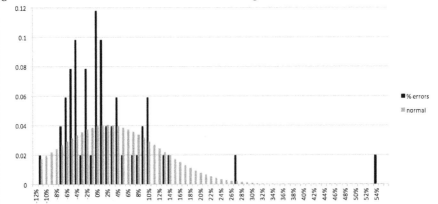

Bounds using the normal approximation would usually be much further apart, in the 1-week example 2000 and 2585 compared to 2132 and 2503. The reason is the occurence of outliers in the percentage errors: there are many small errors and a few big ones, the biggest being 53%. This leads to a relatively high standard deviation and thus wide bounds if the normal approximation is used. It holds more generally that the normal distribution is used in more situations than statistically justified.

---

same way as for the 1-week forecast, using forecasts for moments in the past for which we already know the actuals. We typically see that the precision decreases when the forecasting horizon gets longer and thus the interval gets wider. That is also the case in Figure 3.14, although the space between upper and lower bound fluctuates a little due to randomness (one big error occured in the first weeks we tested the forecast on, and influenced negatively the precision of the forecast for the short forecasting horizon). Still, the difference between the upper and the lower bounds increased from 16% for the 1-week ahead FC to 32% for the 10-week ahead FC. This fact, that we also see when analyzing other call centers, motivates to recalculate forecasts as time progresses as to obtain the highest possible precision.

The bounds thus produced give statistical accuracy. Our method is designed such that, on average in the long run, a certain % of our errors is lower than the lower bound and a certain % is higher than the upper bound. However, this is based on the assumption that the historical data on which the bounds are based is representative for the future. When a trend change occurs of a type that has not been considered when computing the bounds then it might well be the actuals are outside of the bounds consistently. This phenomenon is inherent to forecasting and cannot be avoided.

3.10   Outsourcing contracts

Forecasting often plays an essential role in the relation between companies that outsource (part of) their contacts and the party to which these contacts are outsourced. The usual relation is such that the outsourcer delivers telephone services and the outsourcing company the daily forecast. On the basis of that the outsourcer does the staffing and is usually paid per communication. To avoid bad service for the customer and high costs for the outsourcer the contract usually stipulates a number of situations in which a fine has to be paid. The first one is that, as long as the traffic is within certain defined bounds, then the outsourcer should meet a certain service level. On the other hand, the outsourcing company looses money when the actual traffic is not within the predefined bounds, for example because it always pays for the lower bound, even if there are less calls, or because calls handled above the maximum level are more expensive. It is therefore essential that good forecasts are made and that, when the contract is (re-)negociated, that the right information about forecasting precision, much as we defined in the previous section, is available.

In case only part of the traffic is outsourced we also see other models and possibilities. Sometimes an outsourcer is only hired to offer cheap labor, and the whole WFM process, including workforce scheduling, is being done by the outsourcing company. In the situation where the outsourcer delivers a forecast then the outsourcing company has a number of degrees of freedom, which are not always used in practice. Very often the traffic is split randomly between the internal and the external call center, using some predefined factor (or factors in the case of more than two parties or sites). Changing this factor on the basis of the final forecast or even daily traffic allows to find the right balance between the employment of the internal and the external all center. But it all starts with a good forecast, including its variability.

3.11   Additional information

The forecasting methodology discussed up to know is entirely based on historical call volumes: on the basis of actuals of previous time periods an interpolation to the future is made. In certain call centers the historic call volume can be more precisely estimated using other data sources, such as the number of customers a company has, or the weather. Using this information does not replace the regular forecasting process, but it can be used to improve the precision of the deseasonalized forecast. Certain information will not be available at the moment of forecasting, such as the weather. However, showing such a relation at least shows the boundaries of the precision that can be obtained. Advanced mathematical methods exist to take these extra factors into account.

3.12   Abandonments and redials

Demand forecasting is an activity that can be done separately from capacity planning because demand is not influenced by capacity decisions. This, however, is not completely true. In the long the offered service might lead to changes to changes in demand: a company offering offering bad after-sales service might see a decrease in sales and thus also of service requests. Or a call center that is hard to reach in the afternoon might see a shift to calls in the morning. These gradual changes can be captured in the regular forecasting process.

Something that is harder to capture is the short-term effect of the service level on the call volume. When the service level is low then customer abandon. Part of these caller will redial later on, leading to more calls. This leads to the question: what should we try to forecast and thus get historical data on? Usually we forecast either the total number of calls or the number of calls that got connected. The former probably counts a considerable number of calls multiple times; the latter excludes those callers that did not redial after abandonment. Ideally, one would like to forecast the number of first-time attempts, but in many call centers this information is not available.

We conclude that, especially in the situation where we have data on all calls or all connected calls, the service level might have a considerable impact on the number of calls. For this reason it might be interesting to see which part of the variability in the deseasonalized actuals can be explained by the service level.

3.13   Further reading

An interesting book from the forecasting expert Makridakis that highlights less mathematical issues of forecasting is [21]. Diebold [13] is one of the many books on mathematical forecasting. Linear regression and its extensions are extensively described in most books on statistics. Nowadays it is even possible to obtain free text books, see for example [7].

On the internet, notably Wikipedia, there are many starting points to obtain further knowledge on PDCA, lean management, ISO norms, and so forth.

Chapter 4

The Erlang system

A crucial part of call center performance is understanding the dynamics of a single-skill inbound call center. As the Erlang formulas are often applied in this situation, we call this the Erlang system. This chapter is dedicated to it.

4.1 The Erlang C system

Call centers are complex systems in which technology and human behavior both play important roles. When we want to predict the performance of such a system we cannot take all different aspects into account; we have to make a simplication of reality, a *model*. For the model to be of relevance, it should contain all crucial elements of the system we want to model. The most important features are that call arrival times are unpredictable and that handling times vary. The model having exactly these features is the Erlang C model:

- arrivals according to a Poisson distribution (as discussed in Section 3.1);
- random service duration (which includes talk time and wrap-up time);
- a fixed number of undistinguishable agents (meaning that all agents are, statistically speaking, equally fast);
- all calls wait in queue until they get served (thus no abandonments);
- calls are answered in order of arrival, thus longest-waiting call first.

In this system we are usually interested in the service level (SL), sometimes in the average speed of answer (ASA). For every individual customer the SL objective is met or not. The service level is obtained for a group of callers by taking the percentage for which the SL objective was met. Because of the random fluctuations the SL will be different for almost any group we consider, even when the traffic characteristics are fixed. However, when we take the average over infinitely many calls, then we always get the same number. It is this number that is given by the *Erlang C formula*.

The Erlang C or Erlang delay formula is named after the Danish mathematician A.K. Erlang who derived it at the beginning of the 20th century. The Erlang formula has as input the forecast (FC), the average handling time (AHT), and the number of agents. To compute the SL we also need to know how much waiting time is considered acceptable: the AWT (see page 19). The FC, AHT and AWT are often given in different time units: the FC is often given per 15 minutes, the AHT in minutes, and the AWT in seconds. To avoid confusion it is advisable to use the same units, and to use different notation for that. We will denote the FC per minute with the Greek letter λ. The AHT is denoted with β, measured again in minutes. Now we define the *load a* as $a = \lambda \times \beta$. The load is the amount of agents that would be needed exactly to handle all traffic.

Example *Consider a call center with a FC of 30 per quarter and an AHT of 5 minutes. Then $\lambda = 2$ per minute, and β is 5 minutes. Thus the load is $a = \lambda \times \beta = 2 \times 5 = 10$.*

The Erlang unit

The load is a product of two numbers: one has "minutes" as unit, the other "per minute". Thus the product has no dimension, "minutes" and "per minute" cancel out. We can see this in the example, if we take another unit of time then we still get the same load: the FC is 120 per hour, the AHT is $\frac{1}{12}$th of an hour, and then the load is $120 \times \frac{1}{12} = 10$ again. It is customary to use the unit "Erlang" for the load.

The offered traffic is dealt with by a group of s agents. We assume that the number of agents is higher than the load (thus $s > a$). Otherwise there are, on average, more arrivals than departures per time unit, and thus the number of waiting calls increases all the time, resulting in a SL of 0%. (In reality this won't occur, as callers will abandon.) We can thus consider the difference between s and a as the overcapacity of the system. This overcapacity assures that variations in the offered load can be absorbed. These variations are not due to changes of λ or β, they originate from the intrinsic random behavior of call interarrival and call holding times. Remember that λ and β are averages: it occurs during short periods of time that there are so many arrivals or that service times are so long that undercapacity occurs. The strength of the Erlang formula is the capability to quantify the SL (and other waiting time measures) in this random environment with short periods of undercapacity and therefore queueing.

The Erlang C formula gives the SL for given λ, β, s, and AWT. For the mathematically interested reader we give the exact formula, for $a < s$, and AWT equal to t (also in minutes):

$$SL = 1 - C(s, a) \times e^{-(s/\beta - \lambda)t}.$$

Here e is a mathematical constant, approximately equal to 2.7; $C(s, a)$ is the probability that an arbitrary caller finds all agents occupied, the *probability of delay*. In case $a \geq s$ then $SL = 0$. The formula itself is useful for those who *implement* it; see the box on page 60 for details. For a call center manager or planner it is more important to *understand* it, i.e., to have a feeling for the SL as variables vary. For this reason we plotted the Erlang formula for some typical values in Figure 4.1. We fixed β, s, and t, and varied λ. In the figure we plotted λ on the horizontal axis, and the SL on the vertical axis. The numbers in the figure can be verified using the Erlang C calculator at www.gerkoole.com/CCO.

Example *With $\lambda = 1$ and $\beta = 5$ we have a load of 5 Erlang. Let us schedule 7 agents, and assume that a waiting time of 20 seconds is considered acceptable, that is, AWT = 20 seconds. Filling this in in the Erlang C calculator at www.gerkoole.com/CCO gives a SL of almost 72% (try this!). Increasing the number of agents to 8 already gives a SL of 86%.*

We follow the curve of Figure 4.1 for increasing λ. Starting at 100%, the SL remains close to this upper level until relatively high values of λ. As λ gets such that $a = \lambda \times \beta$ approaches s then the SL starts to decrease more steeply until it reaches 0 at $\lambda = s/\beta = 7/5 = 1.4$. From that point on, as explained earlier, the SL, as predicted by the Erlang formula, remains 0%.

Next to the SL we can also derive the ASA, the average amount of time that calls spend waiting. The overcapacity assures that the average speed of answer remains limited. How they depend on each other is given by the Erlang formula for the ASA. This formula is given by:

$$ASA = \frac{\text{Probability of delay} \times \text{Avg. service time}}{\text{Overcapacity}} = \frac{C(s, a) \times \beta}{s - a}.$$

For the same input parameters as in Figure 4.1 we plotted the ASA in

---

Calculating $C(s,a)$

The most complicated part of the Erlang C calculation is computing $C(s,a)$. The formula is:

$$C(s,a) = \frac{a^s}{(s-1)!\,(s-a)} \left[\sum_{j=0}^{s-1} \frac{a^j}{j!} + \frac{a^s}{(s-1)!\,(s-a)} \right]^{-1}.$$

An experienced programmer will be able to implement this, although one should be careful for numerical instabilities. For example, when calculating $a^j/j!$ for say $a = j = 100$ we divide two extremely big numbers, possibly leading to inaccuracies. Avoiding this is crucial if we want to find the correct answer for the complete range of possible values of a and s.

When the Poisson distribution (see the box on page 28) is already available, as is the case in Excel, then a simpler solution exists. In Excel, the so-called Erlang blocking formula is given by

$$B(s,a) = \text{POISSON}(s,a,\text{FALSE})/\text{POISSON}(s,a,\text{TRUE}).$$

The delay probability C can be computed by using the following formula:

$$C(s,a) = sB(s,a)/(s - a(1 - B(s,a))).$$

This is exactly the approach taken in the simple Excel tool available at www.gerkoole.com/CCO, which can be verified by looking at the underlying VBA code. More information on the Erlang B formula can be found in the box on page 75.

Figure 4.2. We see clearly that as λ approaches the value of $s/\beta = 1.4$ then the waiting time increases dramatically.

The probability of delay is not only an intermediate step in calculating the SL or the ASA, it is also of independent interest: it tells us how many callers are put in the queue and how many find a free agent right away. The probability of delay can also be computed using an Erlang calculator. By computing the SL for an AWT equal to 0 we find 100 minus the delay percentage. Dividing by 100 gives the probability of delay. Thus if we fill in AWT $= 0$, and we can find the delay probability from $100 \times$ probability of delay $= 100 - \text{SL}$.

Example *Now we continue the example. We already saw that the load is 5 Erlang. Let us place 7 agents, then there is 2 Erlang overcapacity. Filling in $\lambda = 1$, $\beta = 5$ and $s = 7$ we find that 68% of the callers waits less than 0 seconds. Thus the probability of delay $C(s,a)$ is equal to 0.32. Now we can fill in the formula for*

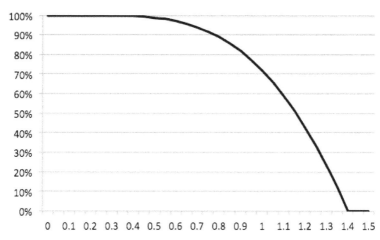

Figure 4.1: SL for $\beta = 5$, $s = 7$, $t = 0.33$, and varying λ

the average waiting time, in seconds:

$$ASA = \frac{C(s,a) \times \beta}{s-a} \approx \frac{0.32 \times 300}{2} = 48 \; seconds.$$

This corresponds with the answers of the Erlang C calculator (be careful with the units, minutes or seconds!). Taking 8 agenten gives

$$ASA = \frac{C(s,a) \times \beta}{s-a} \approx \frac{0.17 \times 300}{3} = 17 \; seconds.$$

Thus increasing the number of agents with 1 reduces the average waiting time with almost a factor 3.

Up to now we just discussed the service level aspects of the Erlang C system. Luckily, the agent side is relatively simple. Let us consider the case that $a < s$, thus $s - a$ is the overcapacity. Because every caller reaches an agent at some point in time, the whole offered load a is split between the s agents. This gives a productivity of $a/s \times 100\%$ to each one of them, if we assume that the load is equally distributed over the agents. If $a \geq s$ then saturation occurs, and eventually agents get calls the moment they become available. In theory, this means a 100% productivity. In practice such a high productivity can only be maintained over short periods of time.

We saw that the Erlang formula can be used to compute the average waiting time for a given number of agents, service times and traffic intensity.

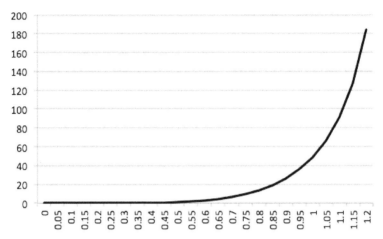

Figure 4.2: ASA for $\beta = 5$, $s = 7$, $t = 0.33$, and varying λ

One would like to use the formula also for other types of questions, such as: for given β and s, and a maximal acceptable ASA or given SL, what is the maximal call volume per time unit λ that the call center can handle? Because of the complexity of $C(s,a)$ we cannot "reverse" the formula, but by trial-and-error we can answer these types of questions.

The question that is of course posed most often is to calculate the minimum number of agents needed for a given load and service level. This also can be done using trial-and-error, and software tools such as our Erlang calculator at www.gerkoole.com/CCO often do this automatically.

Example *In our Erlang C calculator, fill in a FC of 1, an AHT equal to 5, fill in 80 and 20 at SL and select the third scenario. After pushing the "compute" button the computation shows that 8 agents are needed to reach this SL.*

Most software tools will give you an integer number of agents as answer. This makes sense, as we cannot employ say half an agent. However, we can employ an agent half of the time. Thus when a software tool requires you to schedule 17.4 agents during a half an hour, then you should schedule 17 agents during 18 minutes, and 18 agents during 12 minutes. With 17 agents you are below the SL, with 18 you are above. Thus the "bad" SL during 18 minutes is compensated by the better than required SL due to using 18 agents. In our Erlang C calculator we decided not to implement this, because we assume that the time interval is so short that a constant number of agents is required.

The Poisson process

A crucial aspect of the Erlang C formula is that it takes arrivals into account that occur according to a Poisson distribution in any specific interval. Instead of looking at the number in an interval we could also look at the time between two arrivals. For a Poisson distribution these interarrival times have a specific distribution: the so-called *exponential* distribution. A histogram of a sample from this distribution, with average 10 seconds, corresponding to $\lambda = 6$, is plotted below.

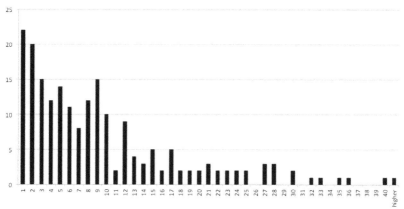

We see many small values, and few very high ones, leading to a relative high standard deviation which is equal to the average (10 seconds in the case of the plot). Actually, the exponential distribution is also assumed to be the law underlying the variability of the handling times. In contrast to the arrival times, there is no practical reason underlying this: the calculation simply requires exponential handling times. An alternative calculation method is simulation, to be discussed later in this chapter.

Example *Let us continue the example. Selecting "Number of agents" instead of "Service level", and pushing the "compute" button again shows that the actual service level is 86% instead of only 80% that was required.*

4.2 Multiple intervals and simulation

There is an interesting contradiction in our use of the Erlang C formula as just described. On one hand, we know that the FC varies from interval to interval, and thus we have to apply the Erlang formula to every interval separately to get the SL or the staffing level for that period. On the other hand, we just saw that the Erlang formula calculates the average performance over an infinite number of customers, and we know that every interval contains only a finite number of calls (the FC plus some Poisson *noise*).

The standard use of the Erlang formula is that we assume that, although it is based on averaging over many customers, it gives a good approximation for shorter periods such as quarters. Performance over longer periods (like a day) can then be obtained by taking weighted averages, where busy intervals (having a higher FC) count heavier than quiet intervals (see also the box on page 19).

The question remains whether the long-term Erlang C formula gives a good estimate for the short-term interval performance approximation problem. An important aspect of this problem is the fact that the number of customers in an interval, and also the handling times, are random, even though the FC and AHT is known. As a consequence, the SL in an interval is also not known beforehand, and can vary randomly. Thus, instead of a single SL, we should perhaps give bounds for the SL, similar to how we produced forecasting bounds in Section 3.9.

Before we go into the details of such bounds and the consequences of it we should quantify the variability. The Erlang C formula cannot help us with that, we have to use *simulation*. With simulation we mimic the behavior of the model, including its randomness, in the computer. Because a single run does not say much (it might as well be a very exceptional one), we have to make multiple runs and draw (statistical) conclusions on the basis of that. In Figure 4.3 we see a histogram of the SL for 100 runs for $\lambda = 10$, $\beta = 3$, $t = 0.33$, and $s = 35$. Erlang C claims a SL of 84%, but the figure clearly show a very high variability, more than half of the 15-minute periods has

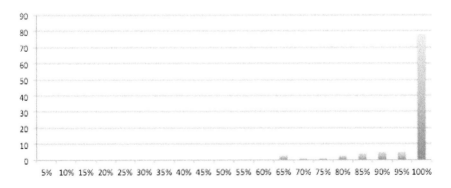

Figure 4.3: Histogram of SL of 100 runs of 15 minutes length

a SL of (almost) 100%! Thus, there are good and bad quarters, quarters where incidentally the call center is congested, and quarters where there is momentarily some overstaffing. This tells us we should not look at the 15-minute level, but probably at a longer time scale. If we would report on a 15-minute time scale, then we will only report randomness.

Let us look next at a longer period, representative for a full day in a call center, of 12 hours. In Figure 4.4 we see that there is much less but still considerable variability. This shows the necessity, even when things go as planned (no big changes in FC or staffing), of *traffic management* or *real-time performance management*. They can make sure, using flexibilty in working hours and task assignment, that the SL is met by the end of the day without too much overstaffing. This is the subject of Chapter 8.

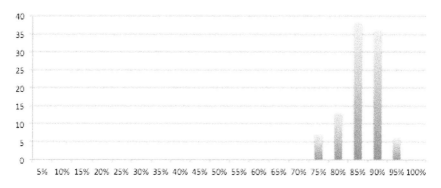

Figure 4.4: Histogram of SL of 100 runs of 12 hours length

Simulation warm-up

When a simulation is started all agents are usually idle, and slowly calls come in, agents start working and after some time queueing can occur. Sometimes this is desirable, for example when we simulate a call center from its opening in the beginning of the day. However, sometimes we want to start the simulation with a full system. This is what we did in the simulation of Figure 4.3, thereby assuming it was some quarter in the middle of the day. If we would have started the simulation empty then around 80% of the runs would have had a SL higher than 95%. Starting with a full system is achieved by letting the system simulate first for some time without measuring. For Figure 4.3 we simulated for 4 hours before measuring for 15 minutes. Of course, this made the simulation 16 times slower.

4.3   Simulating general systems

Simulation proved to be very useful to simulate the Erlang C system for short time periods. We can also use it to change other feautures of the Erlang C model. A reason for exploring alternative models is that the Erlang C formula is known to underestimate the SL, or, equivalently, that it consistently overstaffs. Another reason is the lack of robustness of the Erlang C formula. Take for example a day with 1 period of understaffing, and consider the ASA. Then the ASA prediction for that period is infinite, and so is the weighted average, the daily overall ASA. This is nonsense because the understaffing is only 1 period long. A final reason to change the model is the fact that, as long as we do not model abandonments, we cannot predict them.

Robustness
A model or system is called *robust* if small changes in the input parameters only lead to small changes in the output. An example of a model that is not robust is the Erlang C model. Small errors in for example the FC can lead to big changes in SL and ASA, as we saw in Figures 4.1 and 4.2. Non-robust systems are hard to manage. Most real-life systems are robust or made robust, for obvious reasons. Most call centers are robust. As we will see below, the crucial problem with the Erlang C is that it does not model abandonments. When abandonments are added then the model becomes robust as well.

All three objections against the Erlang C model can be solved (at least to a certain extent) by including abandonments in the model. Once we include abandonments, we have to think about how to model abandonments. As discussed on page 15 in Section 2.2 we assume that every caller has a certain patience: when the patience expires before a call gets assigned to an agent then the call abandons. Using the statistical techniques of Section 2.2 we can determine the patience distribution and make that part of our simulation. Another distribution that we can vary using simulation is the handling time. In Table 4.1 we report on several models that are all changed in one aspect with respect to the baseline Erlang C model. For all models we report the average performance, the variability in SL as shown in the previous section is about the same for all models. In the case of abandonments we have to specify which criterion we are using. For the ASA we use the time a call waits on average in queue, no matter whether it abandons or not; for the SL we use the fraction of all calls that gets answered before the AWT (definition SL_3 on page 23). For comparison we added a scenario in which the FC is 5%

lower.

scenario	abandonments	SL	ASA
Erlang C	–	77.5%/20s	16.4s
$\lambda = 9.5$	–	88.6%/20s	7.4s
constant HT	–	84.0%/20s	8.6s
exponential patience	2.2%	90.6%/20s	4.0s
exp. patience & constant HT	1.8%	92.1%/20s	3.3s
constant patience	0.1%	80.4%/20s	13.1s

Table 4.1: Simulation results for different scenarios with $\lambda = 10$, $\beta = 4$, average patience 3 minutes, and 45 agents

Let us first look at the first three scenarios, without abandonments. Making the handling times all constant, each one of them exactly 4 minutes, improves the SL considerably: from 77 to 84%. Constant handling times are unrealistic, but it suggests that we should also take the form of the handling time distribution into account. For comparison we also added the scenario with 5% less traffic. In that case the SL increases even more, to more than 88%! This shows again the lack of robustness of the Erlang C, and puts the earlier result into perspective: an accurate FC seems to be more important than characterizing the HT distribution (although we can do both of course).

Let us now consider scenarios with abandonments. The first one adds abandonments with exponential patience to the Erlang C model (for information on the exponential distribution, see the box on page 63). We take as average patience 3 minutes, but, due to the variability of the exponential distribution, this still means that some customers abandon quickly: 10% of the callers have a patience of less than 19 seconds. When looking at the results we see that including abandonments has a huge impact on the SL, while the abandonment percentage remains limited, only 2.2%. The reason is that some calls abandon quickly once they get queued and they make space for arrivals behind them, making it more likely that they get served before the AWT. Making the handling times constant now has a much smaller influence. Changing the patience distribution does make a big difference: for constant patience the gain in SL with respect to the Erlang C is very limited. The reason is that the lower values of the patience histogram count most, because the most impatient customers are most likely to abandon. The average patience matters less. We will come back to the choice of the patience parameter in the next section. The conclusion so far is that adding abandonments to the model is crucial and that the handling time distribution is of less importance.

There is an important aspect that we have not addressed yet: redials. Callers who abandon can redial later. To include this into our model we have to characterize redials: what is the probability of a redial, and after how much time does this happen? To answer these questions we need caller information at the call level, including the number that has dialed to identify the caller. Statistical studies show that redials occur relatively quickly after the initial call, but still often in a subsequent interval. That means that the SL in one interval, which determines the number of abandonments, determines partially the numbers of calls in the next intervals. This means that performance calculations become considerably more difficult. Because of the difficulty of both characterizing redials and their performance calculations forecasting and staffing is usually based on the total number of calls, including abandonments.

4.4   The Erlang X system

In the previous section we compared the Erlang C with models with abandonments and saw the advantages of including them. For our calculations we used simulation; while the Erlang C gives the answers immediately, simulation takes a long time to give reliable results. To combine the advantages of both we would need to have a model of which the performance can be calculated instead of simulated and that includes abandonments and possibly more features. The *Erlang X* is such a model.

The Erlang X includes the following features:
- abandonments;
- blocking due to a finite number of lines;
- redials.

The property that makes computation possible is the fact that the time until abandonment has a special distribution: the exponential distribution, which we also used in the computations of Table 4.1. Let us first compare the Erlang X to the Erlang C, thus studying the influence of impatient customers, after which we will look at blocking and redials.

In Figure 4.5 we see that the SL decreases as the FC increases. There are three SL lines, starting at the left at 100%: from top to bottom Erlang X with average patience 1 (the grey line), Erlang X with average patience

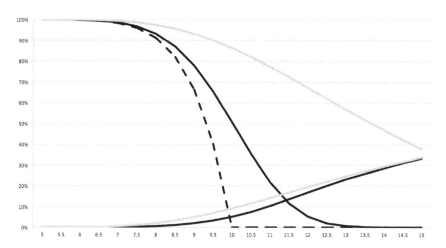

Figure 4.5: SL (decreasing lines) and abandonment percentages (increasing lines) for AHT = 3 min, 30 agents, AWT = 20 s, and average patience 1 (grey line), 10 (black), and ∞ (dashed) minutes, and increasing FC

10 (black), and Erlang C (dashed). The SL under Erlang X is higher because abandonments leave the space for other callers to get served in time; we also see that the Erlang X is much more robust than the Erlang C. It is surprising to see that in overload situations, at the right half of the figure, the SL in the Erlang X system can still be reasonable while the abandonment percentages (the increasing lines at the bottom) are not that high.

Estimating the patience parameter

Estimating the AHT is relatively simple: we average over all handling times (making perhaps a difference between agents and time of day) and use the resulting number as AHT. For the patience it is more complicated. To obtain the distribution of the patience we have to execute a complicated statistical procedure (see page 16), but this does not necessarily help us in estimating the patience distribution. As was said in the previous section, the lower values of the patience distribution count most, but in which way is not clear. A practical solution is fitting the model to the actuals by choosing the patience parameter: on the basis of historical data the value is chosen that makes the Erlang X resemble closest to reality.

In the next figure, Figure 4.6, we want to consider the effect of changes in the number of agents. We took the numbers from Reynolds [26], in which she argues that a single agent can make a big difference, the "power of one". Her calculations are based on the Erlang C model. We see indeed the steepness in the Erlang C model (the steepest line), but the Erlang X models show a much less drastic behavior, although the influence of a single agent can still be quite substantial. Note that the solid lines, the ASA, have their vertical axis on the left; the abandonment percentages have it on the right.

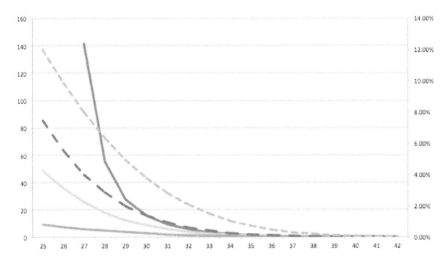

Figure 4.6: ASA (solid lines) and abandonment % (dashed) for FC = 520 per hour, AHT = 3 min, average patience 1, 10, and ∞ min, and increasing number of agents

Next we study the influence of two less often used features of the Erlang X model: *blocking* and *redials*. Blocking refers to the fact that a call is not queued but disconnected. This can have multiple reasons. It can be that the number of lines is bounded, and that there are not enough resources to keep the call connected. Nowadays the number of "trunks" is not really a bottleneck thus this occurs rarely. When a call gets disconnected then it is more likely to be an ACD setting: for costs or quality-of-service reasons the number of customers in the system (in service or waiting in the queue) is limited. The results are plotted in Figure 4.7.

In Figure 4.7 we clearly see the positive effect of blocking: the SL increases significantly as the number of lines decreases. For 30 agents, the black lines, the SL is 50% when the number of lines is almost unlimited; it increases to 98% when there are only 2 waiting places, i.e., 32 lines. It should be noted that in the SL the 10% blocked calls are not counted. If they are considered of not having the SL requirement, then the overall SL is around 89%, still much higher than the 50% without blocking.

Blocking can be seen as a way to avoid long waiting and therefore bad

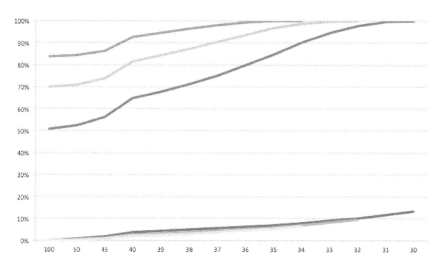

Figure 4.7: SL (above) and blocking % (below) for FC = 10 per min, AHT = 3 min, 30, 32 and 34 agents, AWT = 20 s, average patience 10 min, and varying number of lines

---

Predicting waiting times

In a fully occupied system on average every s/β time units a call is finished. If a call is nth in line, then its waiting time is the time until the nth service completion, which takes on average ns/β time units. For a big call center (or a long queue) this number is quite exact. This can be used to choose the number of lines. For instance, in the numerical example above, a call is finished every 6 seconds. If you prefer to block calls instead of letting them wait 1 minute or more, then we should have no more than 9 waiting places to avoid calls becoming 10th in line and having to wait 60 seconds. By taking 60 seconds as AWT we can indeed verify that less than 4% of the accepted calls spends more than 60 seconds in the queue.

---

service. Thus by blocking a call we avoid that this call receives bad service. This way, blocking can be seen as a favor for a customer who is not aware of the long waiting time. This might be considered an act of paternalism: instead, we could inform the caller about the waiting time and let he or she decide whether or not to abandon. Apart from the technical difficulties in providing such a waiting time estimate, blocking makes space for later arrivals. Thus, by introducing a good blocking policy, we improve the overall SL by forcing abandonment upon customers who have to wait long anyway. Thinking further along these lines, abandoning can be seen as an act of altruism: instead of taking up capacity it makes that later arrivals get service earlier.

Revenue maximization

Blocking can also be used to avoid high connection costs. When the caller is paying for the connection then he or she can stop paying by abandoning; when the call center is paying it can block a call. By studying the ASA for different numbers of lines we can study the influence on the costs.

There are also good reasons not to block a customer: directly, or indirectly, it leads to revenue. In certain situations we can quantify this revenue. If we also know the agent cost per hour availability then we can find the configuration that maximizes the revenue. With the parameters of Figure 4.7, FC = 10 per min, AHT = 3 min and average patience 10 min, and communication costs 10 cents per minute, agent costs 25 Euro per hour, and reward per call 2 Euro, the optimal values are 28 agents and 37 lines (thus maximal 9 calls in queue). These numbers can be reproduced with the Erlang profit calculator at www.gerkoole.com/CCO.

Finally, we consider redials. Redialing is modeled in the Erlang X by adding the average number of abandoned calls per minute to the FC. In Figure 4.8 we clearly see how the SL decreases as the redial percentage increases. When the redial percentage is at 100% all calls get eventually

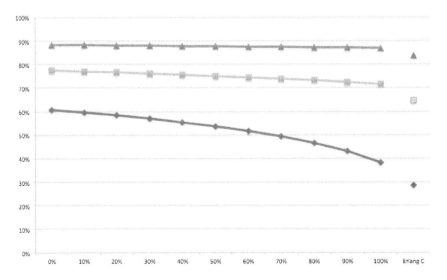

Figure 4.8: SL for FC = 10 per min, AHT = 3 min, 31, 33 and 35 agents, AWT = 20 s, average patience 10 min, and varying redial percentage

served, just as in the Erlang C. However, in the Erlang X calls abandon when there is a long queue and they come back at an arbitrary moment when the queue is likely to be shorter. Therefore the SL of the Erlang X with 100% redials is still higher than the SL of the Erlang C. Note also that we took 31, 33 and 35 agents. For 30 agents or less 100% redials would lead to an unstable system and a 0% SL. All Erlang X computations can be reproduced using the Erlang X calculator at www.gerkoole.com/CCO.

Occupancy

The occupancy for the Erlang C model is easy to calculate, as no calls abandon: $\lambda\beta/s$. When abandonments occur we have to take these into account. Denote with AF the fraction of calls that abandons. Then instead of λ calls per minute, on average only $\lambda(1 - \text{AF})$ call get served. Therefore the occupancy is $\lambda(1 - \text{AF})\beta/s$. The situation gets even more complicated when redials can occur. We first calculate the fraction of first-time attempts that get eventually served. Let's call the redial fraction RF, the total average number of arrivals in the queue (first attempts and redials) I, and the output O. Then $I = \lambda + I \times \text{AF} \times \text{RF}$. Solving this equation for I leads to $I = \lambda/(1 - \text{AF} \times \text{RF})$. We also have $O = I(1 - \text{AF})$. The utilization is given by $O\beta/s$, which is, combining everything, equal to

$$\frac{\lambda \times \beta}{s} \times \frac{1 - \text{AF}}{1 - \text{AF} \times \text{RF}}.$$

Let us check this formula by filling in some known cases. When $\text{AF} = 0$, then we find the occupation of the Erlang C model. When $\text{AF} > 0$, but $\text{RF} = 0$ then we find indeed the occupation of the Erlang X without redials as we just computed. When $\text{AF} > 0$ and $\text{RF} = 1$ then we find again the occupation of the Erlang C, which makes sense, as every customer gets eventually served.

Let us now look at the SL for different levels of the AWT. In Figure 4.9 we plotted the results for different values of AWT and 3 models where the number of agents is chosen such that the SL is around 77%. The first surprising fact is that for the model with little patience, the steepest graph, the number of agents is much lower. We also see that while more customers have to wait, they have to wait shorter, because the graph approaches 100% more quickly than the others. In other words, in the Erlang C system the waiting times are more variable than in the Erlang X.

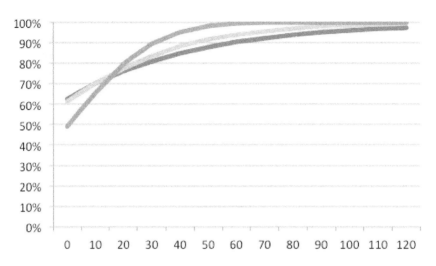

Figure 4.9: SL for FC = 10 per min, AHT = 3 min and varying AWT, for 34, 33 and 28 agents, and Erlang C and Erlang X models with 1 and 10 minutes average patience, respectively

---

Rational abandonment behavior

When we take a closer look at the Erlang C curve in Figure 4.9 then we find that every 10 seconds exactly 19.9% of the waiting calls gets connected, independent of the time a call has already waited. Thus the remaining waiting time is always the same, no matter how long a call has waited. If we look at the Erlang X, then we see that the remaining waiting time gets shorter the longer a call has waited. A consequence of this fact for customers is that one should not abandon while waiting: why hang up after 1 minute if your remaining waiting time is as long or even shorter as when you started waiting? In practice however there are good reasons to hang up after a while. Customers do not know the call center's parameters, and therefore they do not know the average waiting time in the call center. The longer you wait, the more likely you entered a call center with unfavorable parameters, and thus your remaining waiting time does increase.

4.5   Further reading

The Erlang C model is one of the basic models of queueing theory. The graduate-level text book Tijms [37] is one of the sources in which one can find a derivation of the Erlang C formula and the underlying mathematics, such as the exponential distribution and the Poisson process.

J. Anton wrote (with co-authors) a few books on call centers. [4] shows

---

The Erlang B system

A.K. Erlang designed two systems: the Erlang C system and the Erlang B system (the Erlang X system is named after him but developed later). The Erlang B system models asituation without queue: arriving customers who find all resources busy are lost immediately. As such it can be seen as an Erlang X system with 0 patience. It is often used in telecommunication and health care, to compute the performance of nursing wards. It is used now and then also in call centers. One should not mistake the blocking probability B of the Erlang B of the delay probability C of the Erlang C: the latter is always higher because delayed customers have a negative influence on later arrivals.

---

how simulation can be used to improve call center performance. The most interesting part is the description of a number of customer cases. [3] has a title that suggests that it is relevant to WFM, "Call center management by the numbers". However, it is not about call center management. Or, as a Amazon.com customer states in a review: "This book does not cover the fundamentals of call center management; instead it focuses on proving the call center as a valuable component in business. For those that are looking to learn how to manage a call center, this book is not for you."

A.K. Erlang introduced the Erlang model. [8] gives an overview of all his scientific work. Abandonment modeling goes back to another Scandinavian mathematician, the Swede C. Palm [23]. Sze [35] introduced the method for modeling redials that we use in the Erlang X. The revenue maximization model of the box on page 72 is described in Koole & Pot [19].

Chapter 5

Workforce scheduling

This chapter is about scheduling agents in single-skill inbound environments. We discuss different types of scheduling problems, long and short-term issues, different objectives, optimization techniques, and so forth.

5.1   Description of scheduling problems

In the previous chapters we characterized call center demand (forecasting) and we calculated how many agents are required to match this demand (staffing). In this chapter we will see how to schedule agents as to make sure that the staffing requirements are satisfied. In essence it is a mathematical puzzle where we have to schedule the agents in such a way that the staffing requirements are met, that scheduling rules related to agents contracts and legal obligations are satisfied, and all that in such a way that total costs are minimized. The scheduling problem has thus three aspects:
- an objective, which is to minimize the costs of the schedule (for example, by minimizing total agent hours);
- decisions, what are the shifts of the agents;
- constraints that have to be satisfied, being the staffing requirements and the scheduling rules.

Several different versions of the scheduling problem exist, of interest to call centers in different situations. The most often solved problem is where individual agents are scheduled for a week at once. This is an essential part of WFM, as it was introduced on page 2. The reason a week is scheduled at once is that certain staffing rules are often formulated on a weekly level, for example that agents can be scheduled for 5 days of a week. In certain sectors such as health or security it happens that constraints span larger periods, for example that no more than 3 out of 10 weeks weekend shifts are allowed. This happens rarely in call centers, making weeks the longest periods that need to be scheduled at once.

WFM software

Many different WFM tools exist, ranging from inexpensive Excel-based solutions to highly advanced tools that costs 10,000s of Euros/dollars a year. A current trend is that solutions move into the cloud, avoiding the installation of hardware and software at the location of the call center. The major functionality of these tools is agent scheduling, which functions well in general. The quality of forecasting and staffing on the other hand depend highly on the tool. Some of the bigger tools are AC2, Aspect eWFM (formerly TCS), Genesys WFM, Invision, NICE IEX, Teleopti and Verint (formerly Witness/Blue Pumpkin), together scheduling millions of call center agents.

In this chapter we focus on the way agent scheduling can be done, but we should realize that WFM tools have more functionality than just generating good or optimal agent schedules: interfacing with planners and individual agents, and connections with the ACD and for example HR systems are also very important.

There are several other interesting workforce scheduling problems that do not require to work at the agent level, but at the shift level. One is long-term requirements planning. It differs from regular agent scheduling in the fact that shifts are determined, but that no agents are assigned to them. It also differs in the scheduling horizon. WFM shift scheduling is usually done a few weeks in advance; long-term requirements planning can be done months or even years in advance. Its goal is to determine how many agents are needed in the future and it has an impact on the recruitment policy. It should be used in conjunction with workforce planning, in which we determine how many agents we have in the future. Workforce planning will be discussed in Section 5.5.

Planning and scheduling

What is the difference between planning and scheduling? Planning is a general concept about making plans to achieve certain objectives. Planning is a common human activity and is used in almost any possible field. A schedule is a specific type of plan in which resources are assigned to taks. In our case agents are assigned to inbound calls.

Several other shift scheduling problems concern more strategic planning or sales issues. A typical strategic issue is which type of shifts minimize costs. For example, should we hire only agents with full-time contracts or is it better to have a mix of full-time and part-time agents? This type of question can also be answered with shift scheduling methods. Another question, having a similar solution, is what to offer in the situation of an outsourcing party. For a given workload they should evaluate how many agents are necessary to deal with the workload. This requires a similar approach and might also involve different types of shifts.

When making agent schedules it is also conceivable that first shifts are created and that next shifts are assigned to agents. This is a good solution when call centers are small and when the agent requirements are to a large extend similar. It also makes it easier to do the planning with a spreadsheet. In what is next we will concentrate on this type of shift scheduling problems, but first we will discuss the important topic of shrinkage.

5.2 Shrinkage

Unfortunately agents spend less hours on customer contact then what we pay them for. One of the reasons is that sometimes they are available and waiting for a call. All other reasons, including training, paid breaks, illness, and so forth, are together called *shrinkage*. Shrinkage should be added to the staffing level to be sure that enough agents are available for taking calls.

Shrinkage should be accounted for when doing agent scheduling. However, depending on the type of scheduling, different aspects of shrinkage should be added. For example, when doing long-term requirements planning, we should take all aspects of shrinkage, including training and vacations. When doing WFM agent scheduling, these aspects are usually not part of shrinkage, because training is scheduled apart and because people on planned vacations are not scheduled. Also note that the part of shrinkage due to trainings can change from agent to agent, depending on their skills, possibly requiring a different training effort, but also depending on their type of contract: part-time contracts typically have a higher percentage of training, simply because their contract is shorter and the amount of training is usually the same.

Example *A hypothetical single-skill call center has on average weekly 12000 calls, with an AHT of 240 seconds. Let us work with full-time equivalents (FTE) of 40 hours. Then we have a load of $12000 \times 240/(60 \times 60 \times 40) = 20$ FTE. When applying the Erlang formula (to every interval separately!) we find that we*

How to add shrinkage

When there is a shrinkage of $s\%$ it does not mean that we should add simply $s\%$ to the outcome of the staffing calculation. It means that of the agents scheduled on average $s\%$ will not be available. If we write b for the number of agents scheduled, then $b(1-s)$ is the expected number of available agents. This should be at least r (the outcome of the Erlang calculation), which means that b should be equal to $r/(1-s)$, rounded up to the nearest integer.

Next, suppose that there is more than one factor, such as vacation and breaks, that both are part of the shrinkage, and that they account for s_v and $s_b\%$ of the shrinkage. Neither of these effects can be simply added: we should first add agents to account for the breaks, and then for the vacations. Thus the number of scheduled agents should be

$$\frac{r}{(1-s_v)(1-s_b)}.$$

Simply adding the sum of the percentages (that is, $r(1+s_v+s_b)$), what is often done in practice, systematically gives lower staffing levels.

---

need in total 25 FTE (if the shifts were completely flexible). Now we account for the shrinkage: 10% for paid vacations, 7% for illness, 4% for training, 10% for breaks. Doing the calculations correctly (see the box on page 80) gives a requirement of 35 FTE; simply adding the sum of the percentages to the required staffing leads (incorrectly!) to 33 FTE. Covering these staffing with shifts lead to shift inefficiences, including this we find the final result: 37 FTE. (The shift inefficiencies will be the main subject of the next section, they vary considerably from situation to situation.) Thus only 54% of the time that is paid for agents are actually busy with customer service. This number is far from being unrealistic.

Next we look at the shrinkage the moment agents are actually scheduled. It is safe to assume that it is known which agents are available and which are on vacation. We also assume that training is planned and that the breaks are unplanned. This means that only illness and breaks should be accounted for, leading to a requirement of 30 FTE. The actual number of agents scheduled will again be higher, because of shift inefficiencies.

An important aspect of call center management is maximizing the number of productive hours per agent and thus reducing shrinkage and shift inefficiencies. Reducing shrinkage is more the domain of supervisors, shift inefficiencies, which is part of planning, will be an important subject in the remainder of this chapter. Another aspect that is also relevant to planning, but that is often overlooked, is the fact that shrinkage is not constant, but varying. For example, when 30 agents are scheduled and on average 2 agents are ill, then in 25% of the times no agents will be ill at all, and in 15% of the cases 3 or more agents will be ill. Thus shrinkage is subject to variability. How to calculate this variability and how to deal with is the subject of Chapter 8.

Rounding

Most Erlang calculators do rounding. What is meant by this is best illustrated with an example. Take FC = 5, AHT = 3, and 80/20 SL. Then the Erlang formula requires 19 agents. But the SL with 19 agents is 84%. Thus the Erlang calculator chooses the lowest number of agents for which the SL requirement is met, with, as a consequence, a SL higher than the requirement. Next we add the shrinkage, and often we round up to the nearest integer as well. Thus we are twice on the safe side. Alternatively, we could work with non-integer numbers. Some calculators allow that, and their answer is 18.58 agents. This should be interpreted as follows: when you schedule 58% of the time 19 agents and 42% of the time 18, then on average the SL is exactly 80%. Alternatively, we could round to the nearest integer, introducing an error instead of overstaffing.

5.3   Shift scheduling

We start by describing how to solve a relatively simple shift scheduling problem using a spreadsheet. Then we continue discussing more advanced problems. This shift scheduling problem consists of finding the optimal combination of shifts to minimize costs, for a single day in a single-skill inbound call center.

The starting point of shift scheduling are the staffing requirements per 15 or 30-minute interval, obtained from forecasting, staffing and by adding shrinkage. This is the demand that we have to match with supply consisting of agents. Every agent has a shift, and the objective is to find a combination of shifts that exceeds the staffing requirements and that has minimal overall costs, where we assume that every shift has certain costs attached to it. This can simply be the number of working hours in the shift, but it can as well be some other number.

The first step to make an Excel sheet that solves this problem is to put the requirements in rows. See columns B–D in Figure 5.1 for an example. Here we took AHT equal to 4 minutes, SL 80% within 20 seconds, and a shrinkage of 40%. The next step is to represent the shifts in the Excel sheet. We do this

---

Erlang Excel add-ins

For the use in workforce scheduling it is useful to have the Erlang formulas available in Excel. Several Erlang add-ins exists. Two of these
can be downloaded from www.gerkoole.com/CCO. They make it for example possible to compute the service level by calling a function such as
=ErlangC_ServiceLevel(5,3,17,1/3) which computes the SL using Erlang C
with FC 5 per min, AHT 3 min, 17 agents and an AWT of 20 seconds. Further information can be found in the documentation that is part of the Excel
sheets.

---

by putting a 1 in every cell corresponding to a time interval where people
doing this shift are working. Thus, when considering the shift of column H
in Figure 5.1, agents start at 8:00, have lunch at 12:00-12:30, and leave at
16:30. The number on top, cell H1, represents the number of agents in the
shift. The decision to make is how many agents to schedule for each shift,
thus to determine H1:O1. An important point is determining the number of
agents at any interval. This is done using the Excel SUMPRODUCT function. For example, cell F9 has as content =SUMPRODUCT(H1:O1,H9:O9).
(Note that this formula might be different depending on your language and
country settings; see Appendix B.)

The final step is is to change the decision variables H1:O1 as to find the
best solution. Suppose we want to minimize the total number of shifts. In
this case there are multiple optimal solutions, all scheduling enough agents
in each interval, all with a total of 20 scheduled agents. One of them is
shown in Figure 5.1. In the current situation it is easy to find the optimal
solution by hand. Also in more complicated situations it is often possible
to find good solutions by trying different possibilities, and that is also very
instructive. To find an optimal solution advanced mathematical algorithms
exist, which can be called as add-ins from within Excel. One of these solvers
is available for free in Excel, but its functionality is rather limited and even
for relatively simple problems it is not guaranteed to give the optimal solution (see the box on page 87).

If we look at the optimal solution in Figure 5.1, then 239 half hours are required, and 320 are scheduled. That is $(320 - 239)/239 = 34\%$ overstaffing.
This type of overstaffing is called *shift inefficiency*: with the shifts we cannot follow the demand curve close enough. The overstaffing is plotted in
Figure 5.2. There are different ways to avoid overstaffing. One is to allow
for understaffing now and then to compensate the overstaffing. Another
is to use other work, for example outbound, to fill the periods with over-

	A	B	C	D	E	F	G	H	I	J	K	L	M	N	O
1							number	10	0	0	0	2	0	0	8
2	time	FC	Erlang C	plus shrinkage		scheduled									
3	08:00	23.6	6	10		10		1							
4	08:30	27.1	6	10		10		1	1						
5	09:00	28.5	6	10		10		1	1	1					
6	09:30	28.1	6	10		10		1	1	1	1				
7	10:00	31.4	7	12		12		1	1	1	1	1			
8	10:30	31.1	7	12		12		1	1	1	1	1	1		
9	11:00	24.7	6	10		12		1	1	1	1	1	1	1	
10	11:30	24.0	6	10		20		1	1	1	1	1	1	1	1
11	12:00	27.8	6	10		10			1	1	1	1	1	1	1
12	12:30	31.3	7	12		20		1		1	1	1	1	1	1
13	13:00	34.6	7	12		20		1	1		1	1	1	1	1
14	13:30	29.4	7	12		20		1	1	1		1	1	1	1
15	14:00	31.6	7	12		18		1	1	1	1		1	1	1
16	14:30	29.7	7	12		20		1	1	1	1	1		1	1
17	15:00	38.0	8	14		20		1	1	1	1	1	1		1
18	15:30	32.3	7	12		12		1	1	1	1	1	1	1	
19	16:00	23.6	6	10		20		1	1	1	1	1	1	1	1
20	16:30	20.4	5	9		10			1	1	1	1	1	1	1
21	17:00	14.6	4	7		10				1	1	1	1	1	1
22	17:30	15.7	4	7		10					1	1	1	1	1
23	18:00	15.5	4	7		10						1	1	1	1
24	18:30	16.1	4	7		8							1	1	1
25	19:00	12.4	4	7		8								1	1
26	19:30	8.6	3	5		8									1
27	total			239		320									

Figure 5.1: Excel sheet with shift scheduling problem

staffing. A third method is to expand the number of shifts. We will discuss all three types of solutions: the multi-channel approach in Chapter 7, the method with under and overstaffing later in this section, and the method with different types of skills right now.

Let us for example assume that, next to the full-time shifts, there are also part-time shifts of 4 consecutive hours. The costs of these shifts are more than half the costs of a full-time shift, let's say 0.6 compared to 1. Now we can extend the sheet with these new shifts. Optimizing by hand is harder, but after some trying and perhaps using the solver (see the box on page 87) we will find a solution like the one in Figure 5.3. We see that 10 full-time shifts are replaced by 13 part-time shifts, and that overstaffing is reduced to 10%. This is a typical use of shift scheduling outside the area of day-to-day WFM: on the basis of this type of calculations the strategic decision to

---

Mathematical programming

Problems where some goal function has to be optimized with side constraints are called *mathematical programming problems*. Shift scheduling is a typical mathematical programming problem. The mathematical programming formulation (of a slightly more general version) of the problem is as follows:

$$\min \left\{ \sum_{k=1}^{K} c_k x_k \;\middle|\; \begin{array}{ll} \sum_{k=1}^{K} a_{tk} x_k \geq s_t, & t = 1, \ldots, T \\ l_n \leq \sum_{m \in S_n} x_m \leq u_n, & S_n \subset \{1, \ldots, K\}, \; n = 1, \ldots, N \\ x_k \geq 0 \text{ and integer}, & k = 1, \ldots, K \end{array} \right\}.$$

"min" refers to minimization, after the bracket we have the objective, and after the bar the constraints. In the objective we see a summation ($\sum$) with x_k the decision variables denoting the number of shifts of type k, and c_k the costs of shift k, $k = 1, \ldots, K$. Thus the objective is to minimize the total costs. The first constraint contains the following variables: $a_{tk} = 1$ if shift k works in interval t, 0 otherwise; s_t, the number of agents required in interval t. The left-hand side of this equation is the number of agents in interval t, which should be bigger or equal to the number required. The next equation models the fact that a number of shifts has possibly a minimum and a maximum number of agents. This way agent groups with similar contracts can be modeled. The final constraint assures that an integer and non-negative number of agents is scheduled.

Although this formulation looks quite complicated, we saw that it is not that difficult to implement it in a spreadsheet. It is also possible to implement it in other environments, such as a WFM software tool.

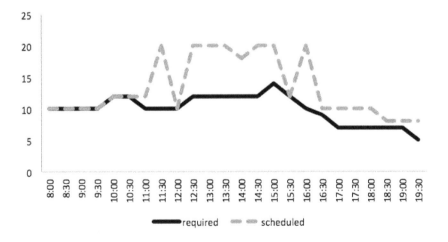

Figure 5.2: Required and scheduled staff with only full-time shifts

work with different contract types can be made. Next, it can help make the decision how many people to hire with a specific type of contract.

	A	B	C	D	E	F	G	H	I	J	K	L	M	N	O	P	Q	R	S	T	U	V	W	X	Y	Z	AA	AB	AC	AD	AE	AF
1	total costs		17.8			number		4	0	0	0	2	0	0	4	6	0	0	0	0	0	0	0	4	0	0	0	0	0	0	2	1
2						costs		1	1	1	1	1	1	1	0.6	0.6	0.6	0.6	0.6	0.6	0.6	0.6	0.6	0.6	0.6	0.6	0.6	0.6	0.6	0.6	0.6	0.6
3	time	FC	Erlang C plus shrinkage				scheduled																									
4	08:00	23.6	6	10			10	1								1																
5	08:30	27.1	6	10			10	1	1							1	1															
6	09:00	28.5	6	10			10	1	1	1						1	1	1														
7	09:30	28.1	6	10			10	1	1	1	1					1	1	1	1													
8	10:00	31.4	7	12			12	1	1	1	1	1				1	1	1	1	1												
9	10:30	31.1	7	12			12	1	1	1	1	1	1			1	1	1	1	1	1											
10	11:00	24.7	6	10			12	1	1	1	1	1	1	1		1	1	1	1	1	1	1										
11	11:30	24.0	6	10			16	1	1	1	1	1	1	1	1	1	1	1	1	1	1	1	1									
12	12:00	27.8	6	10			10		1	1	1	1	1	1	1		1	1	1	1	1	1	1									
13	12:30	31.3	7	12			14	1		1	1	1	1	1	1	1		1	1	1	1	1	1	1								
14	13:00	34.6	7	12			14	1	1		1	1	1	1	1	1	1		1	1	1	1	1	1	1							
15	13:30	29.4	7	12			14	1	1	1		1	1	1	1	1	1	1		1	1	1	1	1	1	1						
16	14:00	31.6	7	12			12	1	1	1	1		1	1	1	1	1	1	1		1	1	1	1	1	1	1					
17	14:30	29.7	7	12			14	1	1	1	1	1		1	1	1	1	1	1	1		1	1	1	1	1	1	1				
18	15:00	38.0	8	14			14	1	1	1	1	1	1		1	1	1	1	1	1	1		1	1	1	1	1	1	1			
19	15:30	32.3	7	12			12	1	1	1	1	1	1	1		1	1	1	1	1	1	1		1	1	1	1	1	1	1		
20	16:00	23.6	6	10			13	1	1	1	1	1	1	1	1	1	1	1	1	1	1	1	1		1	1	1	1	1	1	1		
21	16:30	20.4	5	9			9		1	1	1	1	1	1	1		1	1	1	1	1	1	1			1	1	1	1	1	1	1	1
22	17:00	14.6	4	7			9			1	1	1	1	1	1			1	1	1	1	1	1				1	1	1	1	1	1	1
23	17:30	15.7	4	7			9				1	1	1	1	1				1	1	1	1	1					1	1	1	1	1	1
24	18:00	15.5	4	7			9					1	1	1	1					1	1	1	1						1	1	1	1	1
25	18:30	16.1	4	7			7						1	1	1						1	1	1							1	1	1	1
26	19:00	12.4	4	7			7							1	1							1	1								1	1	1
27	19:30	8.6	3	5			5								1								1									1	1
28	total		239				264																										

Figure 5.3: Excel sheet with shift scheduling problem with full-time and part-time shifts

The method as just described leads to overstaffing and thus to a higher than necessary SL. Reasons are the shift inefficiencies and possibly rounding (see the box on page 81). Even the introduction of shorter shifts does not completely remove this problem. A method that does not require changing shifts is considering the overall daily SL. Thus, we have no (or less restrictive) constraints on every interval, but we require that the SL requirement is met at the overall daily level. Implementing this requires a completely new structure of the Excel sheet, as in Figure 5.4. Because of the shrinkage we need an Erlang formula that can handle a non-integer number of agents. Note that we only work with full-time shifts.

We see that with only 15 shifts we can reach an overall SL of 80.9%. Note that the SL in cell C27 is a weighted average over the interval SL. (See the box on page 19 for more on weighted averages.) Finding the optimal combination of shifts is hard to do by hand; the current solution was found by the Excel solver. Filling in the solution of Figure 5.1, which schedules 20 agents, leads to an overall SL of 93.6%. This is the combined effect of rounding up and shift inefficiencies. Thus by looking at the overall SL we can reduce significantly the number of agents, in the example 25%. The disadvantage is a varying SL, which gets (according to the Erlang C) as low

	A	B	C	D	E	F	G	H	I	J	K	L	M
1					number	7	2	0	1	0	1	1	3
2	time	FC	SL	scheduled									
3	08:00	23.6	52.9%	7		1							
4	08:30	27.1	71.4%	9		1	1						
5	09:00	28.5	65.8%	9		1	1	1					
6	09:30	28.1	81.3%	10		1	1	1	1				
7	10:00	31.4	71.6%	10		1	1	1	1	1			
8	10:30	31.1	81.7%	11		1	1	1	1	1	1		
9	11:00	24.7	96.3%	12		1	1	1	1	1	1	1	
10	11:30	24.0	99.6%	15		1	1	1	1	1	1	1	1
11	12:00	27.8	51.5%	8			1	1	1	1	1	1	1
12	12:30	31.3	93.3%	13		1		1	1	1	1	1	1
13	13:00	34.6	96.3%	15		1	1		1	1	1	1	1
14	13:30	29.4	97.1%	14		1	1	1		1	1	1	1
15	14:00	31.6	97.8%	15		1	1	1	1		1	1	1
16	14:30	29.7	97.0%	14		1	1	1	1	1		1	1
17	15:00	38.0	89.2%	14		1	1	1	1	1	1		1
18	15:30	32.3	87.0%	12		1	1	1	1	1	1	1	
19	16:00	23.6	99.7%	15		1	1	1	1	1	1	1	1
20	16:30	20.4	81.5%	8			1	1	1	1	1	1	1
21	17:00	14.6	76.5%	6				1	1	1	1	1	1
22	17:30	15.7	71.6%	6					1	1	1	1	1
23	18:00	15.5	55.9%	5						1	1	1	1
24	18:30	16.1	52.3%	5							1	1	1
25	19:00	12.4	46.1%	4								1	1
26	19:30	8.6	48.9%	3									1
27	total		80.9%	240									

Figure 5.4: Excel sheet with shift scheduling problem with overall SL constraint

as 46%. An intermediate solution is to add a SL constraint for every interval (e.g., 60%).

5.4   Agent scheduling

The shift scheduling method as we just discussed is a good starting point for agent scheduling. It can be used in different ways, which we will discuss one by one.

In certain call centers all agents have the same type of shift. Then agent scheduling consists of two steps: shift scheduling and assigning agents to

Using the solver

The settings of the solver for finding the solution of Figure 5.4 are shown below. After hitting "Solve", starting from the solution of Figure 5.1, it start searching for the optimal solution. After several minutes it produced the solution of Figure 5.4.

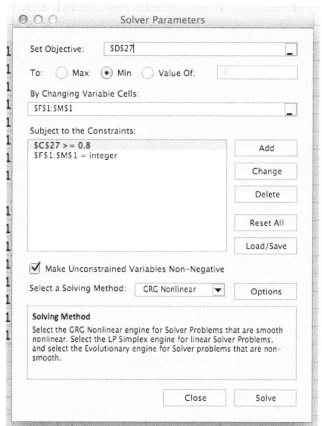

We see that the solver follows exactly the structure of mathematical programming problems (see the box on page 84): objective, variables/cells that can be changed, constraints. Be careful when using the solver, the quality of the solution depends strongly on the type and size of the problem. A background in optimization problems is required to make optimal use of the solver.

shifts. There are different ways to do that, based on priorities of agents for certain hours of the day, or by letting agents make their choices, for examples based on seniority (the longest working agent gets to choose first). An interesting question is when the shifts are made at the weekly level, and all agents should work 5 days in the week. The resulting problem is similar to the shift scheduling problem studied in the previous section, with days instead of 30-minute intervals and a 5-day roster instead of an 8-hour shifts. An example problem is given in Figure 5.5. We assumed that the agents have 2 consecutive days off. The solver schedules 7 shifts more than required. 4 of these are scheduled on Sunday, probably not the best solution. By hand they could be moved to a better day. (It is possible to add a constraint that balances the overstaffing, but mathematically that becomes quite complicated.)

	A	B	C	D	E	F	G	H	I	J	K	L
1					number	11	1	0	3	1	3	3
2	day	required		scheduled								
3	Monday	20		21		1			1	1	1	1
4	Tuesday	18		19		1	1			1	1	1
5	Wednesday	18		18		1	1	1			1	1
6	Thursday	18		18		1	1	1	1			1
7	Friday	15		16		1	1	1	1	1		
8	Saturday	8		8			1	1	1	1	1	
9	Sunday	6		10				1	1	1	1	1
10		103		110								

Figure 5.5: Example Excel sheet with weekly rostering problem

So far we assumed that there is a single type of shift that all agents can do. Next we consider agent scheduling where this is not the case, where there are groups of agents that have different types of shifts. This problem can be solved by using different types of shifts, one for each type of agent contract. To avoid that more shifts of a certain type are planned than there are agents available we should add an upper limit to the number of agents that can be scheduled of a certain type. This can be done without great difficulty in the sheet of Figure 5.3, see also the box on page 84. When we limit the number of available agents, then it might be possible that there is no solution that achieves the SL constraint: there are simply not enough agents. The solver will indicate that there is no feasible solution. A possible solution is the inclusion of overtime, probably at additional costs.

The scheduling can also be done at the agent level instead of the group level, then all kinds of personal preferences can be taken into account. Conceptually it just means that the agent groups have size 1. However, administrating all information in Excel becomes awkward. A software tool where agents can log in to a graphical user interface where they can make changes, see their shifts and so forth is required.

In certain situations even more complexity is required. It regularly happens that agents have flexible contracts in which they work say 24 hours per week, with varying shift lengths, or they have *min-max* contracts, in which their number of weekly working hours lies within a range, say between 24 and 32 hours per week. It is still possible to make daily shifts first and then combine them in a next step to agent rosters, but combined with personal agent preferences this will quickly lead to bad and infeasible agent schedules. An integrated approach, in which the weekly schedule is made at once, is required. This optimization problem is so big and difficult that the Excel solver cannot be used anymore, other methods are required (see the box on page 89).

Optimization methods

When the problem gets bigger and more constraints are added, then the formulation of the form of the box on page 84 get increasingly harder to formulate and to solve using methods that guarantee optimal solutions. Min-max contract and the requirement that trainings take 2 consecutive hours are examples of constraints that are hard to fit in this framework. For this class of problems other optimization methods exist that are faster but that do not necessarily find the optimal solution. These methods, called *heuristics*, are very widely applicable, and constitute also the only viable method in the case of multi-skilled call centers, as we will see Chapter 6.

When all agents need to be scheduled, as is often the case, then the problem amounts to minimizing the costs of the min-max contracts and the overtime. In the case of fixed working hours the costs are fixed. In that situation we could maximize the SL instead of minimizing costs.

Further complexity is added when we add other activities or constraints. We could for example make training part of the shrinkage and do training whenever the SL allows it. We could also schedule training. The way to do this is similar to the way other activities such as outbound and email are scheduled. This will be discussed in Chapter 7. Additional constraints could for example be related to agents having the same shift because of car pooling, a minimum number of agents at periods with low traffic, and so forth.

5.5   Workforce planning

This chapter dealt up to now with the question how to schedule available agents. An equally important question is how many agents to hire and when to make sure we have exactly the right number of agents to meet the schedule requirements. A complicating factor is that it usually takes a few months between the decision to hire agents and the moment they are operational, due to the hiring process and the training. Thus at the moment the decision about the number to hire has to be taken it is unknown how many agents will have left by the time the agents become operational.

Example   *Suppose we have a call center with 500 agents. We have to hire agents right now, which will be operational after three months. We then need a total of 520 agents. Agent turn-over is estimated at 10% on average over a three-month period. How many agents to hire?*

The obvious answer seems to be 70: if we do nothing then three months later 10% of the 500 agents will have left, leaving 450, thus 70 agents are needed to reach 520. However, it would be completely coincidental if exactly 50 agents would have left, much like the arrival experiment in the box on page 30. On top of that, the probability of leaving will certainly not be 10%, because of all kinds of reasons internal and external to the call center, such as the labor market situation. For this reason because 80 agents will be hired, excluding agents not making it through the initial training.

We conclude that fluctuation occur and they cannot be predicted timely enough. Thus, unless other measures are taken, management should decide on which policy to follow: a service-oriented policy in which more agents than needed on average are hired (as in the example), or a cost-oriented policy in which less agents are hired.

5.6   Further reading

The report [20] contains information about the market share of WFM tools.

Every undergraduate text book in operations research contains information about mathematical programming. Two that make also extensive use of spreadsheets are Hillier & Lieberman [18] and Winston & Albright [38].

Chapter 6

Multi-skill environments

In call centers having different types of calls, there is usually a subset of agents capable of handling any specific type of call. When these subsets do not overlap then, from a planning point of view, the call center can be seen as several separate smaller call centers. When the subsets overlap, meaning that certain agents have the flexibility to handle different types of calls, then the performance can be considerable better. At the same time the planning problems become much more complex. The details of these planning problems are discussed in this chapter.

6.1   The possible gains

When a call center grows in size or in the number of different types of tasks then the moment comes that management considers having agents specialized in only a subset of all tasks. There are several reasons for this: specialized agents are more efficient (lower AHT), need less training, and management becomes easier in certain aspects. Moreover, in certain call centers it is impossible that all agents have all skills, for example in call centers offering services in all European languages. Thus there are good reasons to have specialized agents. But there is a price to pay: specialized agents are less flexible. This can potentially lead to a highly inefficient operation, as the next example shows.

Example   *A call center has 10 lines, each with FC 0.2 per minute and AHT 4 minutes. Then each line needs 3 agents to reach an 80/20 SL. If all agents were completely cross-trained, then we would have 1 line with FC 2, and we would need*

91

The division of labour

Adam Smith wrote in 1776, in the first lines of his famous book: "The greatest improvements in the productive powers of labour seem [...] to have been the effects of the division of labour" [33]. However, it is recognized nowadays that in our modern service economy we need also robust production and service systems, which can handle fluctuations. Take, for example, the 3:1 & 1:3 rule, which is part of Lean manufacturing: every worker should know at least 3 skills, and for each skill there should be at least 3 workers having it. This is of course a rule of thumb: depending on the situation is might be optimal to have other numbers than 3.

---

only 11 agents instead of 30! Even if the AHT would increase by 25% to 5 minutes because multi-skilled agents are less proficient and have to switch between tasks then 14 agents would suffice, all according to Erlang C calculations.

The conclusion of the example is that a call center with only specialized agents can be very inefficient. However, it does not mean that all agents should have as many skills as possible, experience shows that a relatively low percentage of cross-trained agents gives most of the potential advantages. Later in this chapter we will discuss in more detail the different aspects of staffing multi-skilled call centers. Staffing in this context means not only deciding the number of agents required, but also their skills.

Technology

Introducing multiple skills can only be done if the ACD can differentiate between the skills. There are different ways to obtain this differentiation. One way is installing a VRU (voice response unit) where callers have to choose; another way is communicating different numbers to the clients, depending on the required skill. Sometimes the ACD recognizes the calling number and differentiates between callers, for example between premium and regular customers, as to give the first group a better SL. This is called a DNIS (dialed number identification service). The result is that there are different queues at the ACD for the different skills. Within a queue calls are usually served on a first-come-first-served (FCFS) service.

Originally ACDs were analog, but nowadays they are usually digital, using internet technology. ACDs are still mostly proprietary, but we see a move towards open source.

It should be noted that good staffing is useless unless *routing* is good. Stated differently, when routing is wrong then more agents then necessary need to be staffed. When calls arrive or when x-trained agents become available often decisions have to be made. These decisions are automatically taken by the ACD, on the basis of rules that are entered by the user. Setting these rules well can entail a structural improvement of call center performance. It is our experience that there is room for improvement in this area in many call centers. When the routing rules are not set right then performance management has a difficult job of maintaining the SL objectives. *Skill-based routing* (SBR) is therefore an important subject of this chapter.

Agent scheduling also becomes considerably more complex in multi-skill call centers: not only the right number of agents should be scheduled, they should also have the right combination of skills. Even for call centers who decide not to use SBR and always function in single-skill mode, multi-skilled agents and thus multi-skilled agent scheduling is relevant: multi-skilled are more flexible to schedule, both when it comes to full single-skill shifts or when skills can be changed during the day. Thus agents might handle one day only skill-1 calls, and another day only skill-2 calls, or they might even change skill during the day. SBR on the other hand means that agents can receive at any moment any type of call out of their skill set.

Finally, having multi-skilled agents offers many possibilities for real-time performance management. In fact, SBR can be seen as an automatic form of RTPM. RTPM should be automated as far as possible. It is further discussed in Chapter 8, in this chapter we focus on multi-skill routing, staffing and scheduling.

6.2 Skill-based routing

Many different routing rules exist. To evaluate these rules there are no formulas available, the only way to do it is *discrete-event simulation*. When simulating we mimic the behavior of the call center including all the statistical assumptions concerning arrivals and handling times in the computer. See Chapter 4 for more details on simulation.

Terminology
We assume that calls enter queues where all calls require the same skill. Agents are organized in skill groups, each characterized by the skills they have. Thus agents from skill group $\{A, B\}$ can serve calls from queue A and B. Terminology might be different depending on the ACD manufacturer, but it can be translated into skills and skill groups.

It is hard to interpret results for call centers with many skills and skill groups. For this reason we start with a number of simple systems with 2 skills and 1, 2 or 3 skill groups. First we introduce the most often used routing rules for a call center with 3 skill groups. Basically, there are two types of moments when calls are matched with agents: when a new call arrives, and when an agent becomes available (because s/he finishes a call or logs in). The former we will call the agent selection or call assignment rule, the latter is the agent assignment or call selection rule. The most often used call selection rules are "longest waiting call" (LWC) and priority rules, meaning that there is an order in the call types such that calls of higher priority are selected before calls of lower priority, no matter how long they have waited. Note that LWC is not equivalent to FCFS, depending on the required skill calls might get answered more or less quickly. This is exactly the reason why priority rules can be helpful: when LWC leads to an unbalance in SL then giving priority to the low SL queue might solve this.

The most often used agent selection rules are "longest idle agent" (LIA) and priority rules between the different agent groups. In the 2-skill situation it might be logical to use single-skilled agents with priority ("single-skill first", SSF). From a SL perspective this is optimal, but it might lead to a higher occupancy of single-skilled agents. All these rules can be tried with the SBR simulation tool at www.gerkoole.com/CCO.

Complexity

The routing rules introduced in this section are simple to implement and understand, but they are not necessarily the best rules. For example, the best rule might be between LWC and a priority rule, depend on the waiting time of the second call in a queue, and so forth. Determining exactly the very best (i.e., optimal) rule is a complicated mathematical problem of high complexity. It is complex because there are so many configurations possible. An optimal routing rule will certainly depend on the number of occupied agents in every skill group. Consider a call center with 10 skills, 10 skill groups with each 10 agents. Then there are $11^{10} \approx 25$ billion configurations. Computing the optimal rule is impossible. And even if we could compute it, it would be infeasible to implement. For this reason we use simpler rules of thumb.

The multi-skill simulation tool at www.gerkoole.com/CCO contains two more routing options: a waiting time threshold and an agent threshold. In call centers it regularly occurs that calls have their primary agent group, but that if waiting time increases they can "overflow" to a second group who might have the required skill as secondary skill. All parameters are summarized in Figure 6.1. AP is short for average patience.

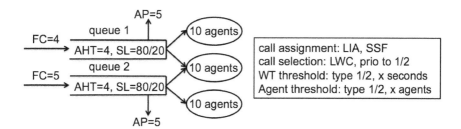

Figure 6.1: Parameters and possibilities for routing policies in a 2-skill call center

The best thing to do is to try out the online simulator for different parameter combinations, and to vary the routing policy to see the consequences. Below we show and discuss a number of common and interesting configurations. First we consider two cases with 1 group of single-skilled agents. The left configuration of Figure 6.2 represents a situation with regular (type 2) and premium (type 1) customers. The right configuration represents a bilingual call center, with a common and a rare language, where all agents speak the common language, and only some the rare language. In both situations the regular LWC/LIA rule gives bad performance, both in terms of SL and in fairness between the agents. Priority rules combined with thresholds give much better performance. Note that in practice, when skill 1 does not reach its SL, often the traffic manager takes a number of multi-skilled agents and puts them in a skill group with only skill 1. This can also be easily simulated: we see that the overall performance is considerably worse than when using a threshold.

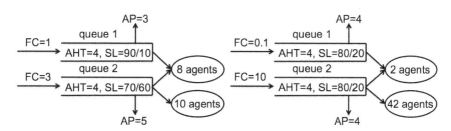

Figure 6.2: Two configurations with two skill sets

It is interesting to change the parameter in the problem with regular and premium calls, especially the FC and the numbers of agents. It is important to find policies that perform well for the most frequently occuring parameter

---

Secondary skills

In the left configuration of Figure 6.2 it can occur, even under good routing rules, that type-1 calls are waiting longer than 10 seconds and that skill-2 specialists are idle. In that case we might want to assign type-1 calls to these agents: the service might be not as good because it is not their preferred skill, but it is better than letting the calls wait even longer. Thus we make a distinction between primary and secondary skills. As a consequence, the number of skill groups increases considerably. Waiting time thresholds are a good way to use secondary skills.

---

combinations.

Let us now consider two examples with 3 skill groups, a small symmetric model, and a larger asymmetric model. We see that the usual LWC/LIA policy does not give equal occupancies, and that priorities might give the reversed situation. Playing with the thresholds solves this problem, but it leads to rather complicated policies. An alternative is using other types of routing policies where waiting at different queue is not treated the same (see the box on page 97).

Routing policies are usually set only once and then used for a long time. For this reason the rules have to be robust. Ideally, the rules should be recalculated every 15 minutes to adapt to the current situation. This would require an automatic mechanism to determine the best routing rule. That raises the question: how to compare two routing rules? If one rule has SL 70/20 and 40/20, and the other has twice 50/20, which one is better? How do we weight SL and occupancy? The same question also plays a role when evaluating long-term call center performance. Note that if forecasts are equal, then 70/20 and 40/20 leads to an overall SL of 55/20. Figure 6.4 gives an example where, in a completely symmetric overload situation, a

---

Robustness

Usually the routing rules are set once and hardly ever changed. However, load and staffing change all the time. Thus, the routing rules should be *robust* in the sense that they should give good results for all reasonable parameters combinations. Good means that they achieve the required objectives. For this reason, it seems reasonable to give the objectives an explicit place in the routing policy. This means that routing should also be based on the overall SL and agent occupancies. To a certain extent Avaya Business Advocate does this already: "The winning strategy is [...] to evaluate overall occupancy to find the least occupied agent who is qualified to handle each call" [1].

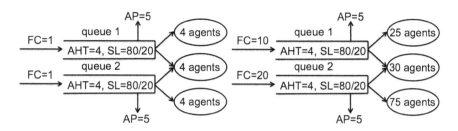

Figure 6.3: Two configurations with three skill sets

More advanced routing rules

The routing rules discussed up to now have only a few options: there is nothing between LWC and a full priority rule. A way to implement a sliding scale is to introduce a factor for each queue and multiply the waiting time with this factor. Now LWC should be adapted such that the call with the highest product of factor and waiting time is selected. As an example, take a call center with B2C and more important B2B calls. Assume waiting time factors are 2 for B2B calls and 1 for B2C calls. Assume that the longest waiting calls have waited 5 for B2B and 15 for B2C. Then, because $2 \times 5 < 1 \times 15$, the B2C calls is served first. If we would have looked 10 seconds later, then the B2B would have been served first because $2 \times 15 > 1 \times 25$. Note that LWC can be reproduced by taking the factors equal and priority rules by taking one factor equal to 0. Note also that we could introduce factors for skill groups in order to balance occupancies.

Another way to obtain a similar result is introducing constants per queue and skill group. When considering which call to take the skill factor should be added to the waiting time, and then the LWC rule should be applied. Similarly, when a call arrives the group factors should be added to the idle times to determine the agent to assign the call to.

---

priority rule gives a higher overall SL than LWC/LIA. Note that this effect would not occur for the ASA or the AE (see page 21). For the AE a symmetric routing rule is better, for the ASA the service order of calls does not matter. This would change if we had single-skilled agents as well.

6.3 Multi-skill staffing

Next to routing, staffing is considerably more difficult in the multi-skill setting than in the single-skill setting. For a single skill we can use an Erlang formula, but for multiple skills there is no formula, we have to rely on simulations. Moreover, we do not only have to determine the right number

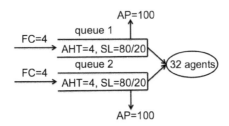

Figure 6.4: A configuration where a piority rule performs best

of agents, we also have decide which skills they should have. The only way how we can use the Erlang formulas is for calculating upper and lower bounds. The minimum total number of agents we need is given by the Erlang formula, applied to the sum of all traffic. (Note that the sum can be made when the AHT are different by taking a weighted average. However, when the AP or the SL are different only approximations can be made.) The total number of agents with a certain skill should at least be the outcome of the Erlang formula applied to that skill. The maximum number is calculated by applying the Erlang formula to each skill and then summing the outcomes.

Example   *Consider the left-side configuration of Figure 6.3. The Erlang X with FC equal to 1 gives 6, with FC 2 11 agents. Thus the minimum total number of agents is 11; the maximum is 12. The number in the skill groups with skills 1 and 1&2 together should be at least 6; the same should hold for 2 and 1&2. This means that a "staffing vector" such as 6 of skill 1, 2 multi-skilled, and 3 agents of skill 2 can be eliminated right away: there are only 5 agents with skill 2, and there should be at least 6. Whether a partition such as 5/1/5 (with 1 the number of single-skilled agents) gives the right SL should be tested by simulation.*

In all our discussions about staffing we assume throughout that routing is done in a good way. This is less obvious than it first appears. One of the properties of good routing is as follows.

Property 1 of good routing: When comparing two staffing configurations, where in one the agents are more "multi-skilled" than in the other, then the performance of the more multi-skilled configuration is better.

This property looks more obvious than it is. It often occurs in call centers that, to compensate for a low SL on one queue, agents are dedicated to that queue by reducing the skills they can take. This is in contrast with the property, meaning that this can only occur in situations where routing is not good.

For the property to hold it is required that the routing rules are adapted to the configuration. This is exactly the reason why skill sets are sometimes reduced: the routing rule is then more adapted to a situation with more single-skill agents. A good routing rule would obtain an even better performance without reducing skill sets.

The goal of staffing is to find a minimal configuration, in the sense that reducing the number of agents or their skill sets would give configurations that do not satisfy the requirements. Often there are multiple minimal configurations. In that case we are interested in finding the best one, which can be done by considering costs for agents in the skill groups. For example, it might be that every additional skill costs 10% in additional costs. This way different configurations can be compared.

Example *We continue with the left-side configuration of Figure 6.3. We saw that it suffices to consider configurations with 11 and 12 agents. With 12 agents we do not need multi-skilled agents: the configuration 6/0/6 obtains the required SL. All other configurations have necessarily more multi-skilled agents. Trying the different possibilities with 11 agents gives 2 minimal configurations: 4/2/5 and 5/2/4. The routing policy is not simple, involving thresholds. In this example we did not consider constraints on the occupancies. For configuration 5/1/5 there is no routing policy for which it achieves the required SL.*

Assuming that single-skill agents cost 1 and 2-skill agents 1.1, we see that configuration 6/0/6 costs 12 and that 4/2/5 and 5/2/4 cost 11.2. Thus both 4/2/5 and 5/2/4 are optimal configurations. Which ons is preferable depends on the availability of agents, which is the subject of the next section.

In the example we saw how to compute the optimal configuration, simply by trying all possibilities. In cases with more than 2 skills this quickly becomes infeasable: there are many different configurations, and their anaysis through simulation takes a long time. Complicated mathematical methods exist to find almost optimal solution in these situations. The technically most advanced WFM packages have these types of algorithms implemented.

6.4   Multi-skill scheduling

Just as in the single-skill situation, there are two ways to do agent scheduling: as a separate step after staffing, or integrated with staffing. Let us first consider staffing as a separate step, and let us generalize the simplest single-skill scheduling problem to 2 skills. We start with staffing, resulting in a good configuration for every interval. The first couple of intervals of an example are shown in Figure 6.5. Note that the total required staffing corresponds to the problem of Figure 5.1.

	A	B	C	D
1		required staffing		
2	time	skill 1	1&2	2
3	08:00	4	2	4
4	08:30	4	2	4
5	09:00	3	3	4
6	09:30	3	4	3
7	10:00	6	0	6
8	10:30	4	3	5

Figure 6.5: Staffing requirements in a 2-skill call center

From the figure it is clear that the shifts can never follow exactly the fluctuations in skill requirements, they are even more volatile than the total number of agents required. It is also not necessary. Thanks to the property on page 98 we can schedule agents with more skills. There is a second property which allows us to schedule more agents than required with less skills. For example, at 9:30 the configuration is 3/4/3; the optimal shift combination schedules 4/3/5. Thus a multi-scheduled agent is replaced by two single-skilled agents (and one more skill-2 agent). This makes performance better, thanks to the following property.

Property 2 of good routing: When comparing two staffing configurations, where in the 2nd an agent of the 1st is replaced by multiple agents having jointly at least the same skill set, then the performance of the 2nd configuration is better.

We will use this property to formulate inequalities that are easy to implement in Excel. To do so, consider the total number of agents with skill 1, with skill 2, and the total. For configuration 3/4/3 this is 7/7/10. The advantage of this representation of the configuration is that every configuration that is better in terms of performance has all number equal or bigger. For exam-

> **Shrinkage**
>
> Adding shrinkage afterwards, as in the single skill case, is not such a good idea, because of the smaller skill groups. Adding the shrinkage for all these skill groups and rounding up can lead to considerable overstaffing. A simple solution is to add the shrinkage to the volume. The best solution, which is however complicated, is to make shrinkage part of the simulation, by simulating the absence of agents, unscheduled breaks, etc.

ple, 4/3/5 becomes 7/8/12, bigger than 7/7/10. This is easy to implement in Excel (for 2 skills, for more than 2 skills this is much more complicated). The full Excel sheet, with only full-time shifts, can be found in Figure 6.6. Columns E–G contains the new representation of the configuration; from column O on we see the schedule, for each skill group; columns K–M contains the scheduled agents; Columns H–J contains the scheduled agents in the new representation. The main constraint is that the values of columns H–J are at least the value of the corresponding cells in columns E–G. The optimal solution is shown in the figure, assuming that multi-skilled agents are 10% more expensive than single-skilled agents. The optimal solution was found using the Excel solver; it is almost impossible to find it manually.

time	required staffing skill 1	1&2	2	req. agents with skill 1	2	1or2	sch. agents with skill 1	2	1or2	scheduled staff skill 1	1&2	2
08:00	4	2	4	6	6	10	6	6	10	4	2	4
08:30	4	2	4	6	6	10	6	6	10	4	2	4
09:00	3	3	4	6	7	10	6	7	11	4	2	5
09:30	3	4	3	7	7	10	7	8	12	4	3	5
10:00	6	0	6	6	6	12	8	9	13	4	4	5
10:30	4	3	5	7	8	12	8	9	13	4	4	5
11:00	3	4	3	7	7	10	8	9	13	4	4	5
11:30	4	3	3	7	6	10	13	14	20	6	7	7
12:00	2	5	3	7	8	10	7	8	10	2	5	3
12:30	5	1	6	6	7	12	13	14	20	6	7	7
13:00	5	2	5	7	7	12	13	13	19	6	7	6
13:30	4	3	5	7	8	12	12	13	19	6	6	7
14:00	4	3	5	7	8	12	12	13	19	6	6	7
14:30	3	5	4	8	9	12	13	14	20	6	7	7
15:00	6	1	7	7	8	14	13	14	20	6	7	7
15:30	3	5	4	8	9	12	8	9	13	4	4	5
16:00	4	3	3	7	6	10	13	14	20	6	7	7
16:30	3	3	3	6	6	9	7	8	10	2	5	3
17:00	1	5	1	6	6	7	7	8	10	2	5	3
17:30	1	4	2	5	6	7	7	7	9	2	5	2
18:00	2	3	2	5	5	7	6	6	8	2	4	2
18:30	2	3	2	5	5	7	5	5	7	2	3	2
19:00	2	1	4	3	5	7	5	5	7	2	3	2
19:30	0	4	1	4	5	5	5	5	7	2	3	2
total	78	72	89	150	161	239	208	224	320	96	112	112
					total	239					total	320
					costs	246					costs	331

Schedule (columns O–AL):

skill	1	1	1	1	1	1	1	1	m	m	m	m	m	m	m	m	2	2	2	2	2	2	2	2
number	4	0	0	0	0	0	0	2	2	0	0	1	1	0	0	3	4	0	1	0	0	0	0	2
08:00	1											1					1							
08:30	1	1										1	1				1	1						
09:00	1	1	1									1	1	1			1	1	1					
09:30	1	1	1	1								1	1	1	1		1	1	1	1				
10:00	1	1	1	1	1							1	1	1	1	1	1	1	1	1	1			
10:30	1	1	1	1	1	1					1	1	1	1	1	1	1	1	1	1	1	1		
11:00	1	1	1	1	1	1	1			1	1	1	1	1	1	1	1	1	1	1	1	1	1	
11:30	1	1	1	1	1	1	1	1	1	1	1	1	1	1	1	1	1	1	1	1	1	1	1	1
12:00		1	1	1	1	1	1	1	1	1	1	1	1	1	1		1	1	1	1	1	1	1	
12:30	1		1	1	1	1	1	1	1	1	1	1	1	1	1		1	1	1	1	1	1		
13:00	1	1		1	1	1	1	1	1	1	1	1	1	1	1		1	1	1	1	1			
13:30	1	1	1		1	1	1	1	1	1	1	1	1	1	1		1	1	1	1				
14:00	1	1	1	1		1	1	1	1	1	1	1	1	1	1		1	1	1					
14:30	1	1	1	1	1		1	1	1	1	1	1	1	1	1		1	1						
15:00	1	1	1	1	1	1		1	1	1	1	1	1	1	1		1							
15:30	1	1	1	1	1	1	1		1	1	1	1	1	1	1									
16:00	1	1	1	1	1	1	1	1	1	1	1	1	1	1	1	1	1	1	1	1	1	1	1	1
16:30		1	1	1	1	1	1	1	1	1	1	1	1	1	1		1	1	1	1	1	1	1	
17:00			1	1	1	1	1	1	1	1	1	1	1	1			1	1	1	1	1	1		
17:30				1	1	1	1	1	1	1	1	1	1				1	1	1	1	1			
18:00					1	1	1	1	1	1	1	1					1	1	1	1				
18:30						1	1	1	1	1	1						1	1	1					
19:00							1	1	1	1							1	1						
19:30								1	1								1							

Figure 6.6: Shift scheduling in a 2-skill call center

On page 85 we saw that integrating staffing and scheduling could reduce overstaffing. The same argument holds in the multi-skill situation. More-over, it avoids scheduling too many multi-skilled agents. The scheduling can right away be done at the agent level. Very sophisticated algorithms are required to solve this combined problem (see also the box on page 89). They involve recursively selecting different solutions and evaluating them by simulation.

Workforce planning

Also workforce planning has multi-skill aspects. However, in contrast with the single-skill case, the focus is not upon hiring, but upon training additional skills. Again, workforce scheduling should give us the desired workforce, in-cluding their skill sets. Taking into account the current workforce and esti-mated turnover should give us the desired training needs.

6.5   Further reading

[1] sheds some light into the functioning of Avaya Business Advocate, a routing system designed to give good robust routing decisions.

Fukunaga et al. [14] give an inside look into the Blue Pumpkin (currently Verint) multi-skill scheduling module by its developers.

Chapter 7

Multi-channel environments

Call centers are sometimes called contact centers: next to inbound calls they often handle email contacts, chat sessions, regular mail and faxes, and outbound calls. These different communication channels offer many possibilities for efficient planning but they pose also some interesting challenges.

Originally, call centers did exactly what their name suggested: handling calls. Other forms of contact, at the time mostly mail and faxes, where handled by different departments. Merging them, together with new emerging channels such as email, had many advantages at the managerial and CRM level. Expertise between departments was shared, and all customer information was aggregated in one CRM system. However, these are not all the advantages. The fact that different channels require different AWT gives flexibility that opens possibilities for efficient planning, at different time levels.

7.1 Single-channel staffing

In this section we first consider the staffing of different types of contacts separately. In the next section we will consider staffing multiple channels together. Apart from inbound we usually see the following channels: email, web forms, mail, fax, chat, and outbound calls. Emails, web forms, mails and faxes have the property that they are asynchronous, i.e., the agent is not busy with the contact at the same time as the customer. Therefore their AWT is much longer than for inbound calls, usually 4–24h for emails and web forms, up to days for mail and faxes. Another form of contact is outbound calling. As it is often in reponse to an earlier contact, there is usually also an

AWT in the order of days. If we use the Erlang C model with a required SL
of for example 90% within 4h we see that the agents are scheduled such that
their occupancy is almost 100%. However, this is an inappriopriate use of
the Erlang C model: the AWT is much longer than the interval for which the
staffing is computed, it is thus not unlikely that the contact is answered in
another interval. But when there are sufficient contacts to be answered, then
we can schedule our agents to work 100% of their available time. When they
should do this is to a certain extend flexible: because of the long AWT work
can be shifted over at least a number of intervals. The amount of time to
be scheduled is the amount of work that is expected to arrive plus possibly
some additional intervals to account for the variability of the work.

Example   *Mail is delivered at 10h in the morning, and the responses are supposed
to be sent in the evening. On an average weekday 110 letters arrive, which take
each on average 6 minutes. This represents on average 22 half hours of work, which
were scheduled throughout the day, especially when shifts overlap. It was found
that often the mails were not finished, and that this was strongly correlated to the
number of letters: when considerably more than 110 letters arrived, then the time
was not sufficient. It was decided to schedule 25 half hours, and that when this is
still not sufficient then it is up to traffic management to find a solution.*

Variability of the amount of asynchronous work

The amount of work from asynchronous channels is variable: both the number
of contacts is variable and their handling times. Because of the nature of the
asynchronous contacts it is of interest to compute the standard deviation of the
total amount of work in a day or a period of a day. There is a mathematical
formula to compute this. Assuming that the forecast is good and that the only
variability in the number of arrivals comes from the Poisson distribution (see
the section that starts on page 27), and that the variability in handling times is
roughly of the same size as the handling times themselves (which is a reasonable assumption), then it is safe to schedule $(FC + 1.4\sqrt{FC}) \times AHT$ instead of
just $FC \times AHT$. Under the assumptions this gives roughly a 84% probability
that all work can be done. If 1.4 is replaced by 2.3 then this probability is 95%.

Chat is a synchronous channel: its AWT is comparable to that of inbound
calls. Thus chat has to be staffed in a similar way as inbound calls. However, again the Erlang formulas cannot be use, because of the fact that multiple chat sessions are handled simultaneously by the same agent. Of course
chats take longer when agents do multiple at the same time, but there are
big advantages in handling multiple chats simultaneously. The reason is

that the agent can answer in one chat while the customers with other ongoing chats are typing. Presumably agents are faster than customers, thus the increase in AHT when handling a few chats simultaneously is expected to be moderate. This is indeed what we find in the data.

Example *In a certain data set we found that the maximum level of parallelism was 3: when all agents handling chat had 3 chat sessions, then the next request was queued. Agents having 1 session had an AHT of 5 minutes, when they had 2 sessions simultaneously then the AHT was 5:33, and with 3 sessions 6:15. This is a big improvement in efficiency. On the other hand, when being one of 3 sessions in parallel, the customer can expect that s/he has to wait 1:15 (6:15−5:00) during the chat session for the agent to be available.*

Different chat calculators can be made, with different levels of sophistication and accuracy. The simplest one is based on Erlang C or X, and uses the fact that the AHT at the highest level of parallelism determines for the most part the SL. This gives a reasonable approximation, especially when the increase in AHT under increasing parallelism is moderate.

Example *We continue the example. Let us assume the FC is 12 per minute. For an AHT of 6:15 we need 83 agents according to the Erlang C formula. Translated to chat, with at maximum 3 sessions in parallel per agents, this means $\lceil 83/3 \rceil = 28$ agents ("$\lceil \cdot \rceil$" means rounding to the next higher integer).*

7.2   Blending

In this section we focus on the short-term effects of handling multiple channels by the same agents, the equivalent of SBR, but in a multi-channel setting. When regarding the occupancy of agents in a regular Erlang C system we see that very often agents are idle. This is confirmed in Figure 7.1, where we see the number of occupied agents in such a system with 6 agents. This opens the possibility to do other work in these idle moments and to improve the productivity. In a multi-channel situation we might want to do outbound calls or emails in the moments that agents are available. However, this should be done in a smart way, otherwise the SL will suffer badly.

It is also possible that (part of) the idle time is filled by tasks that are not customer contacts, such as administrative work. In this chapter we focus on customer contacts. Other activities are discussed in Chapter 8.

We focus on these forms of contact that have an AWT of at least a number of hours, such as emails, faxes or outbound calls. For the asynchronous

---

Predictive dialing

Outbound call centers, mostly used for telemarketing, have problems that are very different from those that handle contacts initiated by the customer. Agent planning is much less of an issue, agents work in general at those times that the probability of response is highest, often early evening when many people are at home. For one specific problem sophisticated planning software exists: for *predictive dialing*. Outbound call centers work with lists of potential customers. In the most basic form each agent gets a list with telephone numbers and starts calling. The disadvantage is that the agent first loses time dialing, then again for waiting, and eventually the call might not be answered. For this reason software exists that does the dialing, and it does so anticipating the times at which agents will be become available. Hence the name predictive dialing. Thus the software uses as input the time it takes to dial, the probability that the call is answered, the number of agents, how many are occupied or free, the AHT, and the number of calls already in process to compute whether or not a new call should be initiated. The objective is to maximize the productivity of the agents, while keeping the amount of *ghost calls* under a prespecified level. A ghost call in this context is a call where a live person answered but without having a agent available to take the call. In certain countries (such as the USA, the UK and Canada) there are laws giving a limit to the percentage of ghost calls.

---

types there are two ways how we can handle them: *preemptive* or *nonpreemptive*. Preemptive means that these contacts can be interrupted, for example for handling an inbound call. Nonpreemptive means that the contact can never be interrupted. Outbound calls can only be handled nonpreemptively, asynchronous contacts can be handled in both ways. Let us start by considering a situation where we have inbound calls and a nonpreemptive second channel, let's say outbound. For simplicity we assume that we have ample outbound calls, and that their AHT is equal to that of the inbound calls. The objective, for a given staffing level, is to do as many outbound calls as possible, under a SL constraint for the inbound calls.

Thus instead of assigning in a static way agents to inbound or outbound calls, they are assigned dynamically to one of the channels. This is known as call blending, as it was originally intended for call center dealing with inbound and outbound traffic. Simply *blending* seems a more appropriate name given the recent focus on communication over the internet. The assignment should be done carefully. An idle agent should obviously be assigned to a waiting inbound call if any are present. But if there are no inbound calls in queue, there is still a decision to make: should we keep the

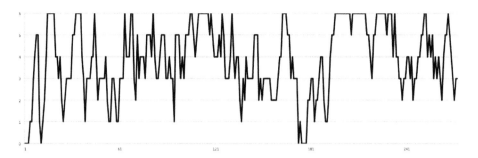

Figure 7.1: Number of busy agents in an Erlang C system with FC $= 1$, AHT $= 4$ and 6 agents

idle agent(s) idle to answer immediately inbound calls as soon as they arrive, or should we assign outbound calls to one or more of the idle agents? A way to maximize productivity is by assigning all free agents to outbound calls. However, then every inbound call has to wait because all agents are always busy. In most situations this will lead to a very low SL. The solution is to keep a number of agents idle for inbound calls when none are waiting. A calculator developed to analyze this situation can be found at www.gerkoole.com/CCO. In the next example it is numerically illustrated how blending can improve productivity while keeping the SL acceptable. Setting the number of agents that have to be kept idle for inbound calls, the *threshold*, is the biggest challenge.

Example   *A call center has* FC $= 5$ *per minute and* AHT $= 5$ *minutes. 30 agents are dedicated to inbound calls to obtain a 80/20 SL, while 5 agents are working on outbound calls. A better performance, a higher SL and more outbound calls served, can be obtained with 33 agents if blending is used, with the threshold, the number of agents held free for inbound calls, equal to 5. Thus blending saves 6% on the workforce in this example.*

In Figure 7.2 we see the situation of the example for various levels of the threshold, compared to the situation of assigning agents once in a static way. We see how a large gain in SL can be obtained with only a small loss in productivity: again an example of decreasing returns.

When preemption is allowed an even better performance is possible. Then the productivity can be 100% while obtaining the SL as if there was no other channel. This can be done by giving every idle agent an inbound call when there is one in the queue, and otherwise another contact, let's say an email. When an inbound call arrives and one or more agents are han-

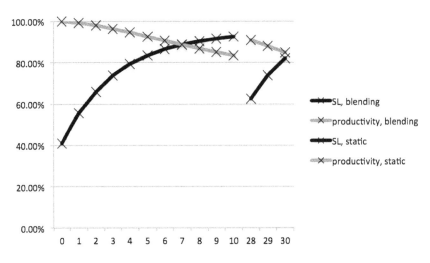

Figure 7.2: SL and productivity as a function of the threshold (blending, left) and number of inbound agents (static, right)

dling outbound, then one of these is interrupted. The disadvantage of this approach is that emails are often preempted, leading to an inefficient handling of emails. Both for reason of agent satisfaction and productivity it is better to interrupt as little as possible. Different approaches to avoid preemption are possible, for example by letting inbound calls wait for an agent to become idle unless they are close to the AWT. Another example, implemented in certain software solutions, is to limit the maximum number of interruptions of an email. Thus, if this maximum is for example set to 3, then an email cannot be interrupted more than 3 times.

Avoiding superfluous switching

An advantage of statically assigning agents is that they can dedicate themselves to a single type of call, inbound or outbound. The disadvantage of blending that all agents do inbound and outbound can be alleviated by assigning some agents to only inbound and some to only outboud. Only a relatively small number of blended agents already gives considerable advantages over completely static, as often we see decreasing returns.

7.3 Multi-channel scheduling

It often happens that, because of lack of appropriate tooling, capacity is planned for asynchronous channels in the same interval as the contacts arrive. This is a missed opportunity: using the flexibility in handling moment that an AWT of multiple intervals gives is an excellent way to reduce the shift inefficiencies that are inherent to inbound calls. In the example on page 82 we obtained an overstaffing of 34% due to shift inefficiency: this can be reduced considerably if we schedule asynchronous channels at the optimal moment, respecting of course the AWT.

We will extend the Excel formulation of the shift scheduling problem in Section 5.3 to include a non-synchronous channel, let's say email. We assume first that the assignment of agents to inbound or email is static, and for simplicity we assume that the AHT is also 4 minutes. The FC for emails is half the FC of inbound, in each interval. The challenge is to find a representation of the constraints: emails should not be handled before they arrive, and not after the AWT (which we take 4h in the example). The first step is realizing that we have to choose the moments at which we schedule agents for handling email. This means more decision variables that have to be changed by the solver if it is used. Deciding if this schedule is *feasible*, i.e., that it is not too early (with respect to the arrival times) or too late (with espect to the AWT) can best be decided by considering the *cumulative* amount of scheduled agent intervals. At every moment the cumulative number should be lower than the cumulative arrivals, and bigger than the cumulative arrivals delayed by the AWT. The Excel formulation for the example is given in Figure 7.3. The first columns are the same as in Figure 5.1. After that the columns have the following interpretation:

- F: forecast per 30 minutes;
- G: required staffing, G3=F3/30*4;
- H: shrinkage is added, H3=G3/(1-0.4). No rounding is done here because agents can handle mail from different intervals in the same interval;
- I: shows H but cumulatively, the numbers show the amounts of work (in agent intervals) that has arrived by that moment. It is not possible to have done more work up to the then indicated. I5=SUM(H\$3:H5);
- J: shows column I but shifted by the AWT, which can be found in H1 (with 30 minutes as unit). The final is the sum over all intervals, because in this particular example we have chosen to finish all emails in the same day;
- K: the cumulative values of the numbers of agents scheduled to handle email, based on column L;

- L: for each interval the number of agents scheduled for email;
- M: the overstaffing, calculated by taking the value in column N minus the values of columns H and L;
- N: the total amount of staffed agents per interval, equal to column F in Figure 5.1. Indeed, the shifts follow in columns P–W.

	A	B	C	D	E	F	G	H	I	J	K	L	M	N
1		inbound				email	AWT =	8 cumulative			scheduled			
2	time	FC	Erlang C	plus shrinkage		FC	required	plus shri	early	late	scheduled	email	overstaffing	total
3	08:00	23.6	6	10		11.8	1.6	2.6	2.6		0.0	0.0	0.0	10
4	08:30	27.1	6	10		13.5	1.8	3.0	5.6		0.0	0.0	0.0	10
5	09:00	28.5	6	10		14.3	1.9	3.2	8.8		0.0	0.0	0.0	10
6	09:30	28.1	6	10		14.0	1.9	3.1	11.9		0.0	0.0	0.0	10
7	10:00	31.4	7	12		15.7	2.1	3.5	15.4		0.0	0.0	0.0	12
8	10:30	31.1	7	12		15.5	2.1	3.5	18.8		0.0	0.0	0.0	12
9	11:00	24.7	6	10		12.3	1.6	2.7	21.6		2.0	2.0	0.0	12
10	11:30	24.0	6	10		12.0	1.6	2.7	24.3	2.6	12.0	10.0	0.0	20
11	12:00	27.8	6	10		13.9	1.9	3.1	27.3	5.6	12.0	0.0	0.0	10
12	12:30	31.3	7	12		15.6	2.1	3.5	30.8	8.8	20.0	8.0	0.0	20
13	13:00	34.6	7	12		17.3	2.3	3.8	34.7	11.9	27.5	7.5	0.5	20
14	13:30	29.4	7	12		14.7	2.0	3.3	37.9	15.4	35.5	8.0	0.0	20
15	14:00	31.6	7	12		15.8	2.1	3.5	41.5	18.8	41.5	6.0	0.0	18
16	14:30	29.7	7	12		14.8	2.0	3.3	44.8	21.6	44.8	3.3	4.7	20
17	15:00	38.0	8	14		19.0	2.5	4.2	49.0	24.3	49.0	4.2	1.8	20
18	15:30	32.3	7	12		16.2	2.2	3.6	52.6	27.3	49.0	0.0	0.0	12
19	16:00	23.6	6	10		11.8	1.6	2.6	55.2	30.8	55.2	6.2	3.8	20
20	16:30	20.4	5	9		10.2	1.4	2.3	57.5	34.7	55.2	0.0	1.0	10
21	17:00	14.6	4	7		7.3	1.0	1.6	59.1	37.9	57.8	2.6	0.4	10
22	17:30	15.7	4	7		7.9	1.0	1.7	60.8	41.5	60.0	2.1	0.9	10
23	18:00	15.5	4	7		7.8	1.0	1.7	62.6	44.8	62.1	2.2	0.8	10
24	18:30	16.1	4	7		8.0	1.1	1.8	64.3	49.0	62.9	0.8	0.2	8
25	19:00	12.4	4	7		6.2	0.8	1.4	65.7	52.6	63.7	0.8	0.2	8
26	19:30	8.6	3	5		4.3	0.6	1.0	66.7	66.7	66.7	3.0	0.0	8
27	total			239				66.7						320
28	overstaffing													4.7%

Figure 7.3: Shift scheduling with inbound and email in Excel

Now the settings for the solver are as follows. The objective is minimizing N27, while changing 2 ranges at the same time: L3:26, and P1:W1. The constraints are: the values in column K should be smaller than the corresponding values in column I and bigger than those in J; the values in column K should be ≥ 0; and the variables P1:W1 should be integer.

In fact, Figure 7.3 already shows the optimal solution, obtained by using the solver. The overstaffing is only 4.7%, while we had 34% in the example of Section 5.3. However, this is not a fair comparison because the amount of traffic is different. To see the effect of the AWT we made calculations where it ranges from 1 (email has to be treated in the same interval) to 24 (no restrictions). In Figure 7.4 we see the results: extending the AWT from 1 to 2 intervals gives the greatest decrease in overstaffing, while the lowest is already reached for an AWT of 7 intervals. The actual shape will differ from case to case, but evidently we will see diminishing returns in all situations.

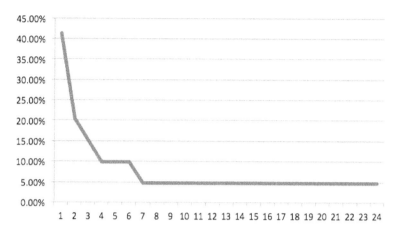

Figure 7.4: Overstaffing as a function of the AWT (measured in 30-minute intervals)

> **Single-channel agents**
> The scheduling problems discussed in this section all assume that all agents are able to do both channels. Sometimes this is not the case or not desirable. In case the optimal schedule does not occcommodate the use of these single-channel agents then we have to schedule for them. This can be done by copying columns P–W two times, for both single-channel types. Additional constraints have to be entered to make sure agents are scheduled for the channel they are skilled for.

Up to now we discussed the situation where agents were either scheduled for inbound or for email. Next we discuss both blending situations: with preemptions and without. In the first the agents can be scheduled up to 100% utilization. The Excel sheet can be changed as follows: column K can be replaced by substracting column D from N. Then we replace the constraint for column K by K should be bigger than L and N should be bigger than D. This leads to solutions with less agents than the corresponding problem without interruptions.

A model that performs between both models discussed is the blending model without preemptions, which has a threshold to keep agents free for inbound traffic. Using appropriate Excel functions this can also be implemented in Excel. However, dus to the non-linearity of the blending model this can quickly lead to search problems in the solver leading to non-optimal solutions.

7.4   Further reading

The formula referred to in the box on page 104 can be found in Ross [28].

Samuelson [30] describes in detail, but without becoming too technical, the functioning of a predictive dialer.

Chapter 8

Real-time performance management

Real-time performance management (RTPM), also known as *traffic manage-ment*, is an essential part of WFM. Because of unforeseen fluctuations SL and occupancy will rarely be as planned. Because of this adaptations to the plan are necessary, by changing the ways in which agents are employed. This chapter is about RTPM, flexibility and their relation.

8.1   Schedule adherence

Changing plans according to the current situation is an important activity, but it makes only sense if we execute our plans (almost) exactly. Schedule adherence measure the extent to which agents follow their schedule: it is the percentage of scheduled time that the agents are available for handling contacts divided by the total scheduled time.

Example   *An agent has an 4 hour schedule, starting with 1 hour of inbound calls, then 1 hour of outbound, a paid 10-minute break, and then again 1h50 of inbound. The agent logs in 10 minutes late, then continues with a call 5 minutes in the email time before switching channel, then delays the break by 10 minutes because she finished an outbound call, and finally finishes on time. Then out of the scheduled 4 hours she was 25 minutes not working on the scheduled activity, leading to an adherence of $(240 - 25)/240 = 90\%$.*

Agents are usually not expected to obtain 100% adherence, the target is often around 95%. This allows agents, for example when switching ac-

113

tivities, to finish a contact without being threathened immediately for not meeting the adherence target. However, this additional time can also be spent on extra breaks, so it does not motivate the agent to finish contacts or to start with a new contact few minutes before the end of the scheduled time. A way around this is to account for work done a couple of minutes after the end of the scheduled time. Although it is hard to determine the right amount of time (see the box on remaining talk time), it is not uncustomary to take half an AHT's length.

Example   *We continue with the example. Suppose that the first 5 minutes after a change of activity are also counted when calculating the adherence. Now 10 more minutes (twice 5) are counted as work time, and the adherence is* $(240 - 15)/240 = 94\%$.

Remaining talk time

When the AHT is on average say 6 minutes, what is then the remaining talk time of a call that is going on when the shift of an agent finishes? The logical answer seems to be 3 minutes, but then we do not account for the variability of the call duration. But that is not the only thing. It is actually more likely that the call with which an agent finishes is longer than average, thus it is even more than 3 minutes on average. To understand this, we will discuss first the so-called *waiting-time paradox.*

Consider a bus that arrives on average every 10 minutes at a bus stop. The time between arrivals is not exactly 10 minutes because of random events, such as traffic density and traffic lights. A passenger regularly takes the bus without looking at the schedule. What is the average waiting time of the passenger? One would expect 5 minutes, but that is not the case. It is longer, because the passenger is more likely to arrive in a longer inter-arrival interval. And, to make things worse, this bus is likely to be more crowded than average!

The situation of the waiting-time paradox is exactly the one of the agent working after the end of the shift. Consider again the situation with an AHT of 6 minutes, and also a standard deviation of around 6 minutes. Then the average remaining time after the end of the shift is not 3 minutes, but again 6 minutes! Prolonging the adherence with half of an AHT covers therefore only part of the time agents spend on their last call.

8.2   Planning with uncertainty

Agent schedules are made several weeks before the day of execution. When making this schedule a number of things that would be useful to known are still uncertain, such as the number of agents that will be absent due to illness, or the weather conditions (who influence the volume in many call centers). Having this information would make our schedules better, but the information arrives too late to base our schedules on. Thus our schedule is based on uncertain information. Usually the average is taken instead of the unknown actual number. When making decisions based on averages, or on incomplete information in general, we do make errors. Dealing with these errors is the subject of this chapter.

WFM is about matching demand and supply. Both are uncertain: the amount of work is uncertain, due to forecasting errors, Poisson variability and also unknown handling times; but also the availability of human resources, due to holidays, illness and so forth is uncertain. It is important to note that the uncertainty decreasing as the day of execution approaches: holidays are planned, special events are known, absences through illnesses become known, and eventually during the day of execution even the occupancy becomes known. This makes it possible to adjust plans on the basis of new information. To be able to do this we must have resource *flexibility*. The different types of flexibility are discussed in the next section.

Definition of uncertainty

Uncertainty has different meanings in different fields. The economist Galbraith [15] defines uncertainty as the difference between the amount of information required to perform a task and the amount of information already possessed by the organization. Uncertainty in probability refers the fact that the outcome of an uncertain or random has an outcome that is not yet determined, that can vary according to its distribution.

Organizations that lack the flexibility to adapt afterwards also have to plan. Planning according to averages without adaptations leads to big fluctuations in performance. The simplest but most costly way to remedy this is to plan according to some worst-case scenario. This is indeed very costly because it results in overcapacity in all but the worst cases.

Organizations that have the possibility to react to current circumstances by using the flexibility of their workforce can obtain better performance for lower costs. However, it makes planning more complicated, and finding the best solution is often a complicated problem. The flexibility can be managed in different ways. An obvious way is having people monitoring demand and supply, and making changes in the planning and scheduling in order to reach the goals of the planning. This is how it is often done in call

> **Flaw of averages**
> Basing decisions on averages without taking variability into account can be dangerous, only very rarely it is optimal to use the average. Take for example someone who wants to cross a river by foot that is on average 0.5 meter deep. The deepest point can well be 3 meters! In this situation it is better to estimate the maximum depth of the river. This and other examples can be found in "The Flaw of Averages" [31], an interesting book about the impact of variability.

centers: *traffic managers* monitor the service levels and the traffic. On the basis of that they make changes in the available resources and the way they are deployed. Another way to use flexibility is having systems that use the flexibility automatically. Skill-based routing and blending are examples. In Figure 7.2 and the accompanying text we saw that, when used in the right way, blending automatically adapts for short-time fluctuations in load on inbound calls. Blending also adapts automatically for forecast uncertainty (forecasting errors), as we sill see shortly. An example of smart automated flexibility at the level of agent availability is that of home workers who are automatically requested to log in when service level is low.

Even though the planning can be adapted to new information, it is important to start with a good initial plan to avoid changes as much as possible. Often one starts with average values of those parameters that are uncertain, such as the daily forecast. This is not necessarily the best solution: when it is cheaper to scale up in staffing then to step down then it might be better to use a level lower than the average as forecast, and vice versa.

8.3   Flexibility

The goal of WFM is to match demand and supply as good as possible. A characterizing feature of call centers is the fact that, especially for inbound calls, supply should follow demand very closely: otherwise waiting times will grow unacceptably, or there is considerable overstaffing. In other industries, even in health care, there is much more time to react to demand fluctuations, and therefore the match between demand and supply is usually much less close.

There are different types of flexibility that allow us to match demand and supply with good quality service (i.e., the right call to the right agent) and acceptable waiting times, even under considerable uncertainty of demand and also supply. (Indeed, part of our shrinkage, especially absence of

---

Demand uncertainty and manufacturing

When we buy a TV we are hardly interested in the conditions under which this set was produced or the time it took; we are interested in the outcome of this process. This is typical for manufacturing. Production proceeds consumption, and inventory is built to be able to handle demand fluctuations. This way customers rarely have to wait for their product, and production can be done in a very regulated homogeneous manner. Crucial for this is the separation of production and consumption.

Customer contact is a service. One of the defining features of services is that the customer is part of the 'production' process: production and consumption occur at the same time. No advance production is possible. This, together with the waiting time requirements of especially inbound calls, makes customer contact, more than any other industry, extremely vulnerable to demand fluctuations.

---

agents, is unpredictable.) We will list the different types of flexibility, and for which types of uncertainty they can be deployed. We have some flexibility in demand (such as the AWT and the possibility to turn an inbound call in an outbound call via a call-back option), but most of the flexibility has to do with the agents.

Shrinkage is random

In call centers we add a fixed percentage to staffing to account for absence, meetings, short breaks, and so forth: *shrinkage*. However, at least part of the shrinkage is random. As an example, at the time of planning, it cannot be predicted how many agents exactly will be ill at a certain day. However, we can compute the probabilities on the basis of its distribution, which is the so-called *binomial* distribution. (We encountered it before, see the box on page 30.) Suppose for example that 100 agents are scheduled and that the random part of shrinkage accounts for 10% of the unavailability. Then we expect 90 agents to be available, but that probability of that happening is only 13% (BINOM.DIST(90,100,0.9,FALSE) in Excel, 0.9 is the probability that agents are available). To have 90 agents with 80% certainty we need to schedule 105 agents (because BINOM.DIST(90,104,0.9,TRUE) is almost 20%).

The different forms of flexibity follow the types of fluctuations we discovered when discussing forecasting in Chapter 3: the seasonal pattern, the weekly and daily patterns, forecasting errors and special events, and finally the Poisson noise.

The longest-term flexibility that we need makes it possible to follow the yearly seasonal pattern. Certain call centers have for example a demand peak around the holidays at the end of the year, which requires flexible contracts that gives the call center the possibility to schedule at the end of the year more agents or existing agents for more hours. Some of this flexibility can also be used for short-term flexibility, for unpredictable peaks. That is, if we have a good procedure for handling short-term unpredictable peaks, then we could also use it for peaks that are known well in advance. However, this advance knowledge allows us to look for a better and less costly solution.

The next form of flexibility is that we have the possibility to make agent schedules that follow the weekly demand pattern. This concerns flexibility that is not part of RTPM, but of agent scheduling as discussed from page 86 on. Depending on the country different ways of scheduling are prevailing, but the bottom line is that there should be sufficient variety in shifts to make an efficient and good schedule possible. A typical problems that occurs often is a lack of flexibility in types of shifts, leading to overstaffing in the middle of the day due to overlapping full-time shifts. Another typical problem is the lack of flexibility in scheduling agents leading to systematic understaffing at certain periods during the week, typically Monday morning (because of high demand) and Wednesday and Friday afternoon and evening (because of agent preferences). Thus the possibility to make agent schedules avoiding inefficiencies and following demand closely is an important form of flexibility.

Also after the initial agent scheduling it is often possible to change employment hours of already scheduled agents or of agents that are not yet scheduled. We can think of overtime, min-max contracts where agents have contracts that allow for a variable number of working hours per week, or simply of hiring temporary workforce when needed.

Next to flexibility in employment hours we have flexibility in the way that agents are deployed to the benefit of customer service. Deployment can be changed up to the second, thus it can used for short-term variability such as the Poisson noise. It starts with the possibility to have non-call center people work in the call center in case of an emergency. Also often management people in the call center (such as supervisors) can take calls when necessary.

Example   *Consider a bank with a stock-trading line. Waiting on the telephone can lead to huge costs for the clients in case of a stock crash, the value of the stock can go down considerably while the callers are waiting. Therefore it is absolutely necessary that the call center assures its SL even in case of a peak in offered traffic.*

Integrating scheduling and RTPM

An ideal WFM tool should take availability and costs of flexible work into account when making agent schedules. Thus the schedule should be made taking the required flexibility into account. Such a WFM tool should not only take the demand forecast as input, but also information about the expected error, at least upper and lower bounds for the forecast, for example the 5 and 95% *percentiles* of the demand. (Thus the probability that the actual is lower than the minimum or higher than the maximum is both 5%.) On the basis of all this information it can make the right combination between fixed and flexible workers. As part of this calculation it will also make the optimal performance management decisions.

This calculation is complicated by the fact that the shrinkage is random: the number of agents absent is also subject to fluctuations. Thus the joint effect of random shrinkage and random demand should be calculated. We should not take a worst-case approach, such as making an upper bound for the staffing level by combining the upper bound for the demand with the upper bound for the shrinkage: then we obtain a bound that is only exceeding in 5% of 5%, which is 0.25% of the cases. Instead we should make a more complicated calculation to arrive at an overall 5% bound.

As an example, consider a call center where at a certain moment in 90% of the cases between 90 and 110 agents are required. Suppose shrinkage is 20%. Then, for 104 agents, the 90% availability interval is [76, 90]. Thus, if we want to be "very" sure that we do not have too many agents, then we should schedule only 104 agents: at most 90 will show up and that is the underbound for the number of agents. Next, we should schedule 44 flexible agents, because with $104 + 44 = 148$ agents we have an availabilty of at least 110. Thus 30% of our agents need to be flexible, to obtain a bound that is met in 99.75% of the cases. (These calculations are based on the so-called *binomial* distribution; see the box on page 117.) More advanced calculations, using normal approximations, show that 112 fixed and 27 flexible agents give 90% bounds.

They assure this by having people not being part of the call center on standby. They are mobilized in case of a peak in offered load.

The next level of flexibility is in assigning tasks to agents. Part of the shrinkage is flexible and can be controlled: meetings can be delayed when demand is higher than expected, or scheduled at moments when staffing is sufficient and SL is expected to be high. Next, there are choices between different skills and channels. This can be changed at the interval level, by assigning agents to certain skills of groups of skills or by assigning agents to channels. This can also be done at a shorter time scale by skill-based routing or blending. The advantage is that these methods are also effective against short-term fluctuations caused by the Poisson noise.

Next to these methods to delay and prioritize certain channels and skills there are methods to change the traffic. In periods of excessively high load we can try to turn inbound into outbound by offering a call-back option. Sometimes this is not optional but forced upon all or part of the callers. Option to increase or decrease the amount of traffic is by offering chat or trying to cross-sell not only on the basis of the customer profile (is it worth trying or not) but also on the basis of the expected loads and current SL.

8.4   Robust systems

RTPM, or traffic management, uses flexibility to counter the effects of short-term fluctuations, mostly involving the day of execution. Traffic managers are usually in charge of making adaptations to the employment and deployment of agents. However, it is not the case that all traffic management should be done manually by the traffic manager. Certain forms of flexibility have to be employed automatically. Examples are blending and SBR: decisions have to be taken so quickly that manual assignments are impossible, or at least highly suboptimal.

Other types of traffic management are often done manually but can be automized leading to potential benefits. Here we can think of the assignments of agents to certain queues or skills during a certain period, typically a few hours. Traffic management can be supported by a workforce management system that not only supports schedule adherence, but also proposes rescheduling on the basis of updated information. In situations where agents work in a multi-skilled or multi-channel fashion, then only the availability should be decided upon by traffic management, the routing or blending mechanism in the ACD should take care of the optimal assignment of customer contacts to agents as to satisfy all SL requirements. However, this often fails to work as required, because routing and blending rules do not adapt to changes in the overall situation. This leads to traffic managers changing the skills in which the agents are logged into, instead of changing the routing rules. As a consequence, the flexibility of the agents are reduced and the overall performance decreases. Instead, routing rules should be improved, in such a way that they adapt themselves to the current situation, as was also observed in the box on page 96.

Example   *Blending is an excellent way to automatically fill the periods with little inbound traffic with outbound. It is also a way to perform traffic management in* *an automatic way. In the table below the situation with and without blending is compared for three scenarios: one base scenario to which staffing is adapted, and those with 10% more and less inbound traffic. For the non-blending case we show the cases with and without traffic management. The parameters are as follows: AHT 5 minutes, AWT 20 seconds, and threshold 3. In the cases with traffic management (the last and the second but last column) we adapted the number of inbound agents as to obtain a 80/20 SL.*

Forecast (per minute)	4	3.6	4.4	4	3.6	3.6	4.4	4.4
Number of agents	30	30	30	25/5	25/5	23/7	25/5	27/3
Blending	yes	yes	yes	no	no	no	no	no
Service level	84%	90%	76%	85%	95%	86%	65%	84%
Output (per minute)	1.7	2.1	1.3	1	1	1.4	1	0.6

We see that blending outperforms all cases, even those with traffic management. The results for blending would have been even better if the ACD could adapt the threshold automatically. Further experiments can be executed with the calculators on www.gerkoole.com/CCO.

Example *Consider the multi-skill example with parameters shown in the left of the figure below.*

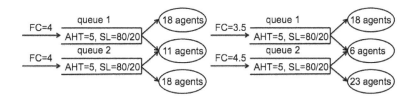

In this situation the SL is 84% for both queues. Now suppose that the FC is wrong, and equal to 3.5 for queue 1 and 4.5 for queue 2. Then the SL, using the LIA/LWC policy of page 94, is 88% and 78%. To balance this, we could do two things: adapt the routing policy, or change the skills of some of the agents. Giving priority to queue 2 gives a more balanced SL of 86 and 81%. Reducing the skills of the multi-skilled agents, as is often done in traffic management, leading to the situation in the right side of the figure, leads to service levels of 81% for both skills. Thus, compared to finding a solution in a different routing rule, traffic management leads to lower service levels.

Another way to assure a good SL under varying conditions is adding a call back (CB) option: once a call enters the queue then the option is given to

---

Improving blending

Certain organizations do not want to implement blending, because it might
lead to frequent fluctuations in channel for individual agents, and because certain agents have a preference for a channel. However, these objections can be
countered by implementing smarter assignment rules. For example, most of
the advantages of blending are obtained by a group of multi-channel agents,
not all agents have to handle all channels. Next, we could restrict the number
of changes between channels, we could for example require that agents do at
least a certain number of contacts in one channels before they might switch to
another channel.

---

be called back at a later moment. A certain percentage of callers will prefer
this option turning them into outbound calls and reducing the number of
customers in queue, leading to a better SL for the other callers. In Table 8.1
results are given from an adaptation to the Erlang C calculation (we assume
that no further abandonments occur). In the first column we see the regular
Erlang C system with no CB. In the 2nd solumn we assume a CB % of 20%.
We also reduced the number of agents by 1 to 14. This leads to a SL of 82%,
higher than under the regular Erlang C system. The SL is computed over
those customer that get served right away, that do not choose for the CB
option. 5.9% chooses for this option, which represents a load of 0.7 Erlang.
Thus the total number of busy agents is less than under the Erlang C and
the SL is higher. We could also impose the CB option to all callers that enter
the queue. In this situation 15 agents in total suffices as well, and the SL
is 100%: nobody enters the queue. Of course, this option is less customer
friendly because the callers have no choice. The remaining 3 scenarios in
the last 3 columns concern the situation with 10% more traffic. We see that
the CB option makes the call center less sensitive to changes in load. This
is because the amount of call backs increases when the load is high: the
demand adapts itself to the supply.

FC	3	3	3	3.3	3.3	3.3
Individual CB %	0%	20%	100%	0%	20%	100%
Number of inbound agents	15	14	13	15	14	11
Overall CB %	0%	5.9%	15.5%	0%	8.7%	29.5%
CB load	0	0.7	1.9	0	1.1	3.9
SL	75%	82%	100%	54%	72%	100%

Table 8.1: Results for callback option with AHT 4 minutes and AWT 20 seconds

Note that the 20% CB probability in Table 8.1 is an arbitrary number. In any particular situation it has to be obtained by experimentation. An alternative to dissuading customers from entering the queue is by limiting its length: for example, we could block calls if the number of waiting customers exceeds 10 calls.

Adaptive cross-selling

Another way to automatically adapt demand to supply, next to the call back option, is adaptive *cross-selling*. Cross-selling is selling additional products to a customer who has called for another issue. Whether or not cross-selling is profitable depends on the customer profile. Thus the cross-selling decision could be taken by the CRM system. We could also base the cross-selling decision on the waiting times. For example, we could try to cross-sell if there are no waiting customers. This leads again to call centers that are robust to parameter changes.

8.5 Manual traffic management

Traffic management, or at least that part of it that is not automated, can be seen as the adaptations made to the plans to achieve the right SL and efficiency objectives by the end of the day. These adaptations concern mostly the employment (working times) and deployment (what are they working on) of agents. Because of the manual nature of traffic management this does not concern changes at the level of contacts, but longer-term changes.

It is important that traffic managers react timely and with the right measures. We start from the situation that at some time during the day the SL from the beginning of the day to that moment is not as required. Which actions should be taken to make sure that by the end of the day the SL is reached? To determine this we have to find out what has been the cause for the SL not being met. Basically, there are two type of causes: the demand is not as forecasted, or the staffing is not as planned. Whatever the reason is for the low SL, we should realize that a low SL will lead to abandonments and redials, thereby increasing the volume later during the day. Thus there are two reasons to increase the staffing levels to beyond what was planned: to compensate for the lower SL in the beginning of the day, and to account for the redials that will occur as a consequence of the bad SL. From this it is clear how important it is to start with a good SL in the beginning of the day. There might be a third reason to staff more than planned. When the reason for the bad SL is that more traffic than expected arrived, then this surge in traffic might well continue during the whole day. This extra traffic requires additional staffing. To determine the amount of extra staffing for the three reasons given no simple formula exists. Data analysis is required to determine abandonment and redial behavior, and also to determine the best way to adapt forecasts in case of significantly higher or lower volume after a few hours. Next, simulation can be used to determine the consequences of new staffing levels. This type of scenario analysis is usually not part of WFM tools.

Changes to the employment of agents are often more expensive and more involved than changes in the deployment. It can also be that changes involve both types. For example, more inbound than expected can lead to more agents doing inbound and less outbound as planned, while the backlog in outbound is handled in overtime. Deployment changes can be separated in two types: those between different queues or channels, and those between call center work and other types of work such as trainings and meetings. The latter part is related to shrinkage: depending on the situation certain parts of shrinkage can be changed, others cannot. Thus shrinkage can be separated in two parts: those aspects that cannot be controlled and are thus outside of the control of the call center, and those that are internal and that can be changed. Illness and mandatory breaks fall in the first category, trainings and meetings in the second.

In the chapter on the Erlang system, in section 4.2, we saw that the load and the SL can fluctuate with no apparant reason. It is therefore important to avoid reacting too quickly to changes in SL.

In this section we focused on the situation where the SL is too low, and traffic management is used to adjust plans to achieve the correct SL. The same techniques should also be used when the SL is too high, and productivity is low. In this situation agents should be sent home when this reduces costs, additional training sessions should be planned, etc.

We finish this chapter, in Table 8.2, with an overview summarizing the types of fluctuations a call center encounters and the forms of flexibility that can be used to counter their effects.

8.6 Further reading

In "Smart Systems" [36] it is argued that all decisions made by frontline workers in an organization are, together, at least as important as the few

flexibility	min-max contracts	task assignment	blending
	agent contracts	overwork	adaptive cross-selling
	temporary workforce	call-back option	SBR
fluctuations	demand: trend	agent availability	
	weekly demand pattern	demand: Poisson noise	
	demand seasonality	daily demand pattern	
	agent turnover	FC errors & events	
	long term		short term

Table 8.2: Overview of sources of fluctuation and forms of flexibility, ranging from long to short term

strategic decisions made by top management. Making these operational decisions smarter, by automating them (partially), is an often underestimated way to make organizations perform better.

More information on the binomial distribution can be found in any introductory level book on probability theory (such as Ross [29]) or online at Wikipedia.

Avaya Business Advocate [1] is a system that is designed to do traffic management in a robust, automated way.

Chapter 9

Analytics

So far this book described a rational approach to workforce management. It is characterized by an extensive use of data and advanced computational methods. This approach can also be used to optimize other aspects of the call center. For example, it can be used to optimize the quality of the contact itself. In this chapter this approach to call center optimization, often called *Business Analytics* (BA), is described and some starting points for analysis are discussed.

9.1   Business analytics

Business Analytics is a rational, data-driven approach to decision making and business planning. It consists of two parts: *Business Intelligence* (BI) and the actual Business Analytics (BA). BI is about measuring business performance: it consists of collecting data, often in a so-called *data warehouse*, making it available through smart IT methods and then using data analysis and statistics to report on business performance. BI is therefore completely focused on past performance. BA uses the outcomes of BI to predict and plan the future. Keywords are forecasting, predictive modeling, and optimization. Simply *Analytics* is often used instead of *Business Analytics*.

BI has proven to be a big economic success, most medium and large companies have BI software. Analytics is also a very succesful approach, with Google as the best known example (their analytics solution is an example of what is known as *web analytics*). Examples of BA are everywhere in Google software, from their revolutionary search algorithm to the way they maximize advertisement revenue by showing ads you are most likely to be

---

A new science?

Business Analytics large uses old well-established methods: it is to a large extend a combination of statistics and *Operations Research* (OR). The examples in the authoritative book "Competing on Analytics" [11] speak for themselves: they are mainly from OR. What is new and interesting about BA is the extensive use of data. The more data-driven approach to statistics is called *data mining*, and also in parallel to the optimization methods of OR several methods were developed of which their usefulness was not proven mathematically but by testing them on large data sets.

---

interested in.

That many believe that BA will grow even bigger is witnessed by the fact that most big consulting firms focus more and more at BA, sometimes under the name of *big data*. Within BA several subfields come into existence: web analytics, marketing analytics, fraud analytics, and so forth.

It is also interesting to note that BA can be used to improve business processes (think of all kinds of planning applications) but also to improve the product itself (such as the Google search algorithm). Traditional applications are more focused on business process improvement, while we see over the last decade an increasing number of applications aimed at improving existing products and inventing new ones.

As the use of BA is increasing, we see that organizations get more advanced in their use of BA. More and more organizations move from just reporting (BI) to forward looking (BA): from a dashboard to a cockpit. In fact, call centers are traditionally an area where BA techniques are used extensively: WFM tools are an excellent example of BA. All steps in BA, from data collection through forecasting to predictive modeling and optimization, are present in WFM tools.

9.2   Workforce optimization

Next to logging all events in the ACD call centers usually record all calls and other customer interactions. All this data together is an excellent source for understanding and improving the performance of the call center. *Workforce Optimization* (WFO) aims to do so. WFO can be seen as a collection of services, sold as an integrated software solution, that has data collection and analytics as its core functionality. It encompasses WFM, and next to WFM it consists of quality monitoring, and possibly agent performance management, e-learning, customer surveying, and so forth.

WFO starts with recording all customer interactions and by logging all events. Call recording is often necessary for legal reasons, but it is also essential for improving the quality of call handling. This is often done by listening back to calls in a training session, but analytics gives the possibility to do this in an automated way using technologies such as *text mining*. Calls can be transformed into text first using *voice recognition*. Through text mining one can automatically look for patterns and phrases in calls. Though not completely accurate, it can be used to access automatically the friendliness of an agent by the occurence of certain words, to adherence to scripts by looking at the occurence of certain phrases, and so forth. It really becomes worthwhile when one starts to connect this type of information with other types of data such as conversion data: then one can start improving the outcomes directly and one can even measure the results of these efforts. Finding this type of relations in the data is called *Workforce analytics*.

9.3   Workforce analytics

To improve performance it is crucial to have information on the overall quality of calls, preferably at the individual call level, but at least at agent level. Basically there two different ways to collect data. The first is by measuring the results directly, for example by measuring the profit per call, or by measuring the reconnect rate per agent, which is a good measure for the FCR ratio. The second is by asking the customer afterwards about the quality of the call. The most popular way to do this is by calling back after the call for a customer satisfaction survey. The number of questions can even be restricted to one, as in the *Net Promoter Score*.

Now we can compare the performance between different agents, and possibly explain differences between agents and calls by analyzing different properties of agents or calls. Consider the relation between quality and handling time. Data from a Dutch call center shows a negative correlation between quality and handling times, see Figure 9.1. Quality is measured as a number between 0 and 100: the higher the better.

In [17] it is suggested that the quality being higher for shorter calls might come from the agent being in charge of the call. One can also think of situations where calls with a simple question are both short and of high quality. The complexity of the call is then a *confounding* variable: it leads to both short calls and high quality, without there being a causal relation between

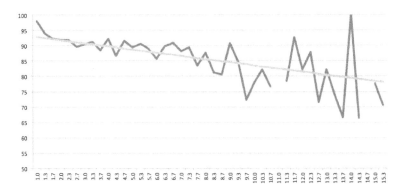

Figure 9.1: Quality as a function of handling times (in minutes) and regression line.
Data obtained via Auditio

length and quality. Note that the fluctuations for higher handling times
come from the lack of data, they are statistically insignificant.

One might expect a similar relation between handling times and reconnects, but this need not be the case. In Figure 9.2 we see both the reconnect
probabilities as a function of the handling times and the handling time histogram.

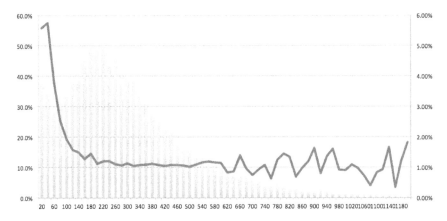

Figure 9.2: Reconnect ratio as a function of handling times (in seconds, line, left
axis) and handling time histogram (bars, right axis). Data from Vanad Laboratories

The handling times in Figure 9.2 have a *bimodal* distribution: there is a
peak around 0 and one around 3 minutes. This suggests two different types
of calls. More insight into the nature of this difference is given by the fact

that the reconnect probability is very different for the two peaks: it is more than 50% for short handling times, and around 10% for higher handling times. To better understand the nature of the short calls we could study them in detail, perhaps by listening back to a number of them. An alternative approach is to see if they are customer or agent-related. In Figure 9.3 we see the relation between AHT and reconnect percentage. We immediately see that there is a negative correlation between AHT and reconnect ratio: the more time the agent takes on average, the higher the FCR ratio and thus, presumably, the better the quality. Note that this is different from what we found for the call center in Figure 9.1, there the quality decreased in the AHT.

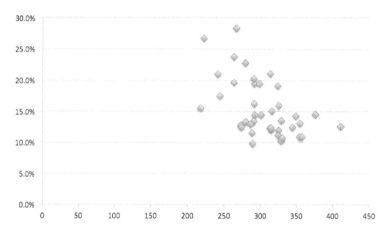

Figure 9.3: Reconnect ratio per agent as a function of AHT (in seconds). Data from Vanad Laboratories

Numbers such as the ones in Figure 9.3 are reason to look deeper into the data and find the causes of the variability in performance. They do not necessarily say that certain agents are underperforming: there can be many reasons for the differences, such as different call types, working hours, and so forth. Note that in the figure a single queue was considered, thus the differences cannot be explained by a difference in skill mix. And even when certain agents are performing not as good as others then analytics can help identify the underlying causes. This is exactly what the idea behind *data mining* is: analyzing data for yet unknown relations that help understand the performance.

On the value of PI's

By measuring performance indicators such as the reconnect rate we hope to learn to understand what drives these indicators, making it possible to push them in a favourable sense. However, we should understand that our Pi's capture only partially our goals. Indeed, overall objectives such as "customer loyalty" or "customer lifetime profit" are hard to connect directly to call center PI's. And even if we try to maximize an easy to meaure PI such as total revenue in a profit center, then it does not suffice to maximize revenue per call: conversions are often the consequence of multiple interactions, thus a profit-less contact might have a big impact on a future conversion.

We should therefore be careful with recklessly pursuing the maximization of a single or a few PI's. Putting a bonus on a low AHT will push agents to cheat and disconnect unfinished calls, leading to customer dissatisfaction and reconnects (making this practice visible!). Similarly, if we steer only on profit maximization then agents will push customer to purchases that are not in their interest, eventually leading to dissatisfaction and future loss of revenue. Striking the right balance between agent motivation through bonuses and overall customer satisfaction is important.

9.4 Call center optimization

There are many call center decisions that go beyond WFM and agent performance, the two main ingredients of WFO. Often they have to deal with optimizing customer interaction, how and where information is available on web sites, which channels are offered, and so forth.

Example *A web shop has limited resources for offering a chat option on its website for browsing customers. Therefore, it should only be offered to customers with the highest potential revenue. A data mining algorithm is used to determine whether this is based on location, department, or any other customer attribute that is available. (To identify customers cookies can be used or customer log-in information.) An advanced algorithm might even use a combination of attributes to identify the most profitable customer.*

Sometimes the data does not tell us the optimal answer to a question. Then we have to generate evidence on a certain issue. By offering to customers different ways to interact with the call centers we can compare statistically different outcomes. Customers are selected randomly but consistently: once option A has been selected for a customer then this option will be used for all interactions. This way of comparing two alternatives is called *A/B testing*, it is used frequently by many companies to improve step by step customer interaction.

Example *The web shop from the example above is not sure about the added value of offering chat: it allows customers to ask additional questions and hereby delays and sometimes even prevents conversion. During a certain period customers were selected randomly whether or not they were offered the option. Now the added value of chat could be estimated, even differentiated over different customer attributes such as departments within the web shop. On the basis of this a rational choice could be made.*

Othr examples where A/B testing can be useful include measuring the impact of a new IVR sciript or different call avoidance strategies. These techniques are still rarely used in call centers, especially when we compare it with the abundant use of WFM software. Nevertheless, their use potentially has a huge impact on customer service and call center performance. Data mining and optimization deserves to be used more often in call centers.

9.5 People

Call center optimization requires people with the right knowledge and skills for their jobs. Of the people concerned with call center optimization some should only be aware of the possibilities, other should of course have a thorough understanding of analytical methods for call center planning.

Higher management and call center managers should be aware of the possibilities of call center analytics. This enables them to communicate with more technical people involved and to understand the improvement possibilities. There are two groups of people who need to have a more thorough knowledge of call center analytics: the people involved in workforce management and the (internal or external) consultants or business analysts working on data mining and analytics as part of improvement projects. The big difference is that planners and forecasters are part of an operational planning cycle and that business analytics work on different projects every time. This requires different skills and knowledge.

Especially with people involved in WFM, forecasters, planners and traffic/performance managers, we see a lack of relevant knowledge. This lack is partly due to the absence of trainings or schools where future planners are educated. It is also the case that their managers often do not see the reason for them to have more background knowledge. Many people concerned have the idea that knowing how the software works and having some spreadsheet knowledge is sufficient to be a good planner. Planners are indeed often quite skilled with the WFM tools they work with, but background knowledge is often lacking.

The requirements for consultants and business analysts are more demanding. While planners regularly execute the same type of task, analysts should be able to conduct varying analytics projects independently. This requires a different level of education and thorough knowledge of relevant techniques from statistics, data mining and optimization. Good analysts usually have a master in operations research, industrial engineering, statistics, or similar. Many even hold a PhD in one of these fields.

9.6   Further reading

Davenport & Harris [11] gives a general description of the possibilities of analytics.

Ayres [5] is a well-written popular-scientific book on data mining and analytics. It contains an accessible description of A/B testing.

Bibliography

[1] How to balance business goals with Avaya Business Advocate, 2011. http://www.avaya.com/uk/resource/assets/brochures/Business%20Advocate%20Gcc0467%20Final.pdf.

[2] O.Z. Akşin, M. Armony, and V. Mehrotra. The modern call-center: A multi-disciplinary perspective on operations management research. *Production and Operations Management*, 16:665–688, 2007.

[3] J. Anton. *Call Center Management by the Numbers*. Purdue University Press, 2007.

[4] J. Anton, V. Bapat, and B. Hall. *Call Center Performance Enhancement Using Simulation and Modeling*. Purdue University Press, 2000.

[5] I. Ayres. *Super Crunchers: Why Thinking-by-Numbers is the New Way to be Smart*. Bantam Books, 2007.

[6] M. Bodin and K. Dawson. *The Call Center Dictionary*. CMP Books, 2002.

[7] D. Brink. *Essentials of Statistics*. bookboon.com, 2010. Free download from http://bookboon.com.

[8] E. Brockmeyer, H.L. Halstrøm, and A. Jensen. The life and works of A.K. Erlang. *Transactions of the Danish Academy of Technical Sciences*, 2, 1948. http://oldwww.com.dtu.dk/teletraffic/Erlang.html.

[9] B. Cleveland. *ICMI's Call Center Management Dictionary*. Call Center Press, 2003.

[10] B. Cleveland and J. Mayben. *Call Center Management on Fast Forward*. Call Center Press, 1997.

[11] T.H. Davenport and J.G. Harris. *Competing on Analytics: The New Science of Winning*. Harvard Business School, 2007.

[12] K. Dawson. Workforce management: The Witness Systems interview. *Call Center Magazine*, May 2006. Interview with Bill Durr, `http://www.icmi.com/Resources/Articles/2006/May/Workforce-Management-The-Witness-Systems-Interview`.

[13] F.X. Diebold. *Elements of Forecasting*. Thomson, 4rd edition, 2007.

[14] A. Fukunaga, E. Hamilton, J. Fama, D. Andre, O. Matan, and I. Nourbakhsh. Staff scheduling for inbound call centers and customer contact centers. *AI Magazine*, 23(4):30–40, 2002.

[15] J. Galbraith. *Designing Complex Organizations*. Addison-Wesley, 1973.

[16] N. Gans, G.M. Koole, and A. Mandelbaum. Telephone call centers: Tutorial, review, and research prospects. *Manufacturing & Service Operations Management*, 5:79–141, 2003.

[17] P. Harts. *The Relation between Quality and Average Handling Time*. Auditio, 2007. In Dutch. Online available at `http://publications.onlinetouch.nl/5/37/#/0`.

[18] F.S. Hillier and G.J. Lieberman. *Introduction to Operations Research*. McGraw-Hill, 8th edition, 2005.

[19] G.M. Koole and S.A. Pot. A note on profit maximization and monotonicity for inbound call centers. *Operations Research*, 59:1304–1308, 2011.

[20] DMG Consulting LLC. Contact center workforce management market report reprint, 2012. `http://www.nice.com/sites/default/files/nice_2012_wfm_report_reprint_final_june_2012.pdf`.

[21] S.G. Makridakis. *Forecasting, Planning, and Strategies for the 21st Century*. The Free Press, 1990.

[22] J. Milner and T. Olsen. Service-level agreements in call centers: Perils and prescriptions. *Management Science*, 54:238–252, 2008.

[23] C. Palm. Methods of judging the annoyance caused by congestion. *Tele*, 4:189–208, 1953.

[24] S.G. Powell, K.R. Baker, and B. Lawson. Impact of errors in operational spreadsheets. *Decision Support Systems*, 7:126–132, 2009.

[25] P. Reynolds. *Call Center Staffing*. The Call Center School Press, 2003.

[26] P. Reynolds. The power of one in call center staffing. `http://www.callcentrehelper.com/images/penny_webinar_power_of_one.pdf`, 2011.

[27] A. Rosenberg. Best practices in workforce management. *Call Center Magazine*, May 2005. `http://www.icmi.com/Resources/Articles/2005/May/Best-Practices-in-Workforce-Management`.

[28] S.M. Ross. *Introduction to Probability Models*. Academic Press, 7th edition, 1997.

[29] S.M. Ross. *A First Course in Probability*. Prentice Hall, 6th edition, 2002.

[30] D.A. Samuelson. Predictive dialing for outbound telephone call centers. *Interfaces*, 29(5):66–81, 1999.

[31] S. Savage. *The Flaw of Averages: Why We Underestimate Risk in the Face of Uncertainty*. Wiley, 2012.

[32] J. Seddon. *Systems Thinking in the Public Sector*. Triarchy Press, 2008.

[33] A. Smith. *An Inquire into the Nature and Causes of the Wealth of Nations*. Digireads.com, 2009 (first published in 1776).

[34] R. Stolletz. *Performance Analysis and Optimization of Inbound Call Centers*. Springer, 2003.

[35] D.Y. Sze. A queueing model for telephone operator staffing. *Operations Research*, 32:229–249, 1984.

[36] J. Taylor and N. Raden. *Smart (Enough) Systems*. Prentice-Hall, 2007.

[37] H.C. Tijms. *A First Course in Stochastic Models*. Wiley, 2003.

[38] W.L. Winston and S.C. Albright. *Practical Management Science*. Cengage Learning, 4th edition, 2012.

All scientific call center publications by the author can be found at the call center publications page of www.gerkoole.com.

Appendix A

Glossary

abandoned call A call that is interrupted by the customer that initiated the call before contact with an agent was made. See also redial.

algorithm A step-by-step method to solve a certain, often computational, problem.

ACD *Automatic Call Distributor*, a part of a PABX that can distribute calls that arrive on one or more numbers to extensions which are part of one or more groups that are assigned to that number.

AE *Average Excess*, alternative service level definition, defined as the average time calls wait beyond the AWT.

agent An employee who works in a call center. Also called (call center) representative ('rep'), or CSR (customers sales representative).

AHT *Average Handling Time*, the time agents spend on average on a call. Includes the wrap-up time.

analytics Also known as *business analytics*, a fact-based approach to business process and product improvement using advanced mathematics and ICT.

ANI *Automatic Number Identification*, a technique used to identify customers by their telephone number. Used in combination with CTI to show right away customer information on the agent's computer screen.

ASA *Average Speed of Answer*, the average time a call waits before speaking to an agent.

AWT *Acceptable Waiting Time*, the target upper bound to the waiting time, very often equal to 20 seconds. Also called Time to Answer (TTA) and Service Time (ST).

B2B, **B2C** *Business-to-business, -consumer*, relative to sales to customers that are businesses resp. consumers.

call blending A way of handling inbound and outbound calls at the same time by assigning them in a dynamic way to agents.

call center A collection of resources (typically agents and ICT equipment) capable of delivering services by telephone.

cost center From Wikipedia: "In business, a cost centre is a division that adds to the cost of an organization, but only indirectly add to its profit. Typical examples include Research and Development, Marketing and Customer service."

channel In the context of contact centers a means to have contact with customers. Examples are telephone, fax, and internet.

contact center A collection of resources (typically agents and ICT equipment) capable of delivering services through multiple communication channels.

CRM *Customer Relationship Management*, mainly used to denote computer systems that allow to record and retrieve interactions with the customer. CRM systems made the advent of call centers possible.

cross-trained Denotes an agent who has more than one skill, who can therefore handle more than one type of call. A **generalist** is *fully* cross-trained. Also denoted as **x-trained**.

CTI *Computer-Telephony Integration*, the process that enables communication between and integration of telephone equipment and computer systems.

data mining A field of science aimed at discovering relations in data. It has a big overlap with statistics, but it is less mathematical, having its origins in computer science.

DNIS *dialed number identification service*, part of the ACD that recognizes the calling number.

FCR *First Call Resolution* applies when a call is handled right the first time, not necessitating a second call. The FCR rate is the fraction of first calls for which this is the case. See also **reconnect**.

FCFS *First Come First Served*, refers to the orders in which queued calls are served: in the order of arrival.

generalist An agent who has all skills, i.e., (s)he can handle all types of calls.

ICT *Information and Communication Technology*, technology relative to computers and technology-assisted communication.

IVR *interactive voice response*, part of an ACD that allows a customer to enter information by responding to instructions through the keypad of the telephone or voice recognition.

LIA *longest idle agent*, an agent selection rule used in multi-skill call centers.

LWC *longest waiting call*, a call selection rule used in multi-skill call centers.

model Used in this book as *mathematical model*, a description in mathematics terms of part of a system, that allows an analysis of certain aspects of that system. For example, a simulation model.

noise Informal statistical term meaning unexplained variability (as in *Poisson noise*).

occupancy The time that an agent is handling calls (talk time plus wrap-up) divided by the total time that the agent is available for handling calls. **Utilization** and **productivity** are nowadays often used as synonyms.

OR *Operations Research*, the science that uses mathematical models to improve business operations. Also known as *Management Science*, therefore sometimes called OR/MS. See also www.informs.org.

planning The organizational process of creating and maintaining a plan (Wikipedia).

PABX *Private Automatic Branch eXchange*, the telephone switch local to the company.

predictive dialer Functionality of an ACD that allows outbound calls to be automatically initiated, anticipating future availability of agents.

productivity See **occupancy**.

reconnect The fact that a caller, after having been served, calls back after some time for the same service. See also **FCR**.

redial The fact that a caller, after having abandoned or being blocked, calls back after some time for the same service. See also **abandonment**.

retrial The fact that a caller, after having been served or not, calls back for the same service. Comprises of **redials** and **reconnects**.

RTPM *Real-time performance management*, the activity having as goal on the day of execution to take actions as to obtain the required SL as good as possible.

scheduling The process of deciding how to commit resources between a variety of possible tasks (Wikipedia).

SBR *Skill(s)-based routing*, the fact that different types of calls are routed to different agent groups based on the type of the call and the skills of the agents.

shrinkage The fraction of time that an agent is not available for taking calls because of holidays, training, paid breaks, etc.

skill group A group of agents all having the same skill set.

skill set The set of skills that an agent or group of agents have.

SL *Service Level*, an somewhat ambiguous term that can relate to all aspects of service (waiting time, abandonments, and so forth). In call centers usually defined as the percentage of calls answered within the **AWT**. Quality of Service is a synonym of the former meaning.

SLA *Service Level Agreement*, the contract between a business unit and higher management or an outsourcer with its client company concerning the required service levels.

SSF *single skill first*, an agent selection rule used in multi-skill call centers, that assigns calls to agents with the least number of skills.

ST *Service Time*, see **AWT**.

specialist An agent who can only handle one type of call. It can also mean an agent who can do even the most difficult calls, in contrast with a generalist. To avoid ambiguity it is better to use the term **single-skilled agent**.

Traffic Management Synonym to **Real-time performance management**.

TTA *Time To Answer*, see **AWT**.

utilization See **occupancy**.

VRU *Voice Response Unit*, synonym to **IVR**.

waiting time The time a call spends between entering the queue (often after a recorded message, or after having made a choice in a VRU) and an agent being connected to the call.

WFM *Workforce Management* consists of all activities from forecasting and planning to online control that have to do with the employment of agents in call center.

WFM tool A computer tool that assists planners with their WFM tasks. It minimally consists of forecasting, Erlang C, and agent scheduling modules.

WFO *Workforce Optimization* includes WFM, call monitoring and agent performance management.

wrap-up time Time after the end of a call that the agent spends on the call. Consist usually of entering call-related data in a computer system.

x-trained Synonym to cross-trained.

Further reading

The list just given is short and only explains most technical terms used in this book. For exhaustive call center dictionaries see [6, 9].

A Dutch-language call center dictionary can be found on the internet at www.callcenterwoordenboek.nl.

Appendix B

Excel

B.1   International use of Excel

Depending on the language and settings of Microsoft Excel formulas might differ. For example, the formula

$$=\text{SUMPRODUCT(B2:B5,D2:D5)/SUM(B2:B5)}$$

would become in Dutch, with a decimal comma,

$$=\text{SOMPRODUCT(B2:B5;D2:D5)/SUM(B2:B5)}.$$

The name of the function is different and the separator between arguments becomes a semicolon to avoid confusion with the decimal separator. Certain names of functions vary between different versions of Excel. In this book we use the English names with a decimal point. Thus international users should change the formulas according to their Excel settings. Tables with names of functions in different languages can be found on the internet.

B.2   Limitations of Excel

Spreadsheets in general, and MS Excel especially, are excellent tools for quickly making complicated calculations. They have a range of built-in functions and add-ins that make it useful in many different application areas. However, Excel has less structure that other environments that have similar functionality. Moreover, it lacks a database, making that data fills unstructured spreadsheet pages. For these reasons one is more likely to

145

make errors in Excel, especially if the same Excel sheet is used repeatedly and by different people. Thus Excel is good for supporting for example the once-off decision to use part-time shifts, done by a business analyst; it is much worse for weekly planning in which different planners adapt every week an existing sheet to varying forecasts and agent availability. Using colors, named ranges and other possibilities of Excel it can be adapted to a certain extent, but it remains less suitable. The result is a loss of time in the long run and an increased possibility of errors. Scientific research in this area shows surprisingly high occurences of errors in Excel sheets. For this reason it is advised to move operational tasks, which are often done repeatedly, away from Excel.

B.3   Further reading

Powell et al. [24] and other papers by the same authors report on statistical studies into the errors in spreadsheets.

CPSIA information can be obtained
at www.ICGtesting.com
Printed in the USA
BVHW040722151118
533165BV00008B/315/P

9 789082 017908